the greener meadow

THE LOCKERT LIBRARY OF POETRY IN TRANSLATION

Editorial Advisor: RICHARD HOWARD

For other titles in the Lockert Library, see p. 272

the greener meadow

Luciano Erba   *Selected Poems*

TRANSLATED BY PETER ROBINSON

PRINCETON UNIVERSITY PRESS

Princeton & Oxford

Italian texts copyright © 2006 by Luciano Erba
Copyright © 2007 by Princeton University Press
Requests for permission to reproduce material from this work should be
sent to Permissions, Princeton University Press

Published by Princeton University Press, 41 William Street, Princeton, New Jersey 08540
In the United Kingdom: Princeton University Press, 3 Market Place,
Woodstock, Oxfordshire OX20 1SY

The Italian texts are reproduced with gratefully acknowledged permission from
Luciano Erba, *Poesie 1951–2001*, edited by Stefano Prandi, published by
Arnoldo Mondadori Editore S.p.A., Milan (2002), and Luciano Erba, *L'altra metà*,
introduced by Stefano Verdino, published by Edizioni San Marco dei Giustiniani,
Genoa, in a series edited by Giorgio Devoto (2004).

All Rights Reserved

LIBRARY OF CONGRESS CATALOGING-IN-PUBLICATION DATA

Erba, Luciano, 1922–
[Poems. English & Italian. Selections]
The greener meadow : selected poems / Luciano Erba ; selected, introduced,
and translated by Peter Robinson.
p. cm. — (Lockert library of poetry in translation)
English and Italian

ISBN-13: 978-0-691-12763-7 (cl : alk. paper)
ISBN-10: 0-691-12763-8 (cl : alk. paper)
ISBN-13: 978-0-691-12764-4 (pbk. : alk. paper)
ISBN-10: 0-691-12764-6 (pbk. : alk. paper)
I. Robinson, Peter, 1953– II. Title. III. Series.
PQ4865.R3A2 2006
851'.914—dc22   2005056514

British Library Cataloging-in-Publication Data is available
This book has been composed in Adobe Caslon

Printed on acid-free paper. ∞

pup.princeton.edu
Printed in the United States of America

1 3 5 7 9 10 8 6 4 2

The Lockert Library of Poetry in Translation is supported by a bequest from
Charles Lacy Lockert (1888–1974).

contents

translator's preface

You can still read, and hear it said, that poetry is what gets lost in translation. The reason given, unsurprisingly, is that languages are not homologous—neither at the levels of syntax and meaning, nor, above all, at the level of sound. It's as if we were being told that poetry would only be translatable if it didn't need translating. Yet this evident lack of congruence between languages is the premise upon which the meeting of sensibilities that is poetic translation must be founded. A poem reconstituted in another language will inevitably have undergone a process of being both lost and then found in translation. The translator has to experience embarrassment, shame even, at this loss, so as to be motivated to help effect the poem being found again elsewhere.

That there are bound to be conflicts of responsibility—conflicts between, broadly speaking, the sense of the original and the sound of the translation—will not so much be what thwarts the poet translating as the very thing that drives the need for ingenuity and invention. As, in their different ways, many poets understand, constraint is the forcing house of creative discovery. I prefer translations that stick as close to their originals as possible, but which nevertheless aim to read as poems in their new language. Indeed, it seems to me that such a balancing of responsibilities is the crucial requirement for a translation to have taken place. Everything else is likely to be more or less well-meaning travesty. Naturally, how a reader responds to such alternative styles of rendering will in part depend upon how the secondary text is presented.

The imitation or version that substantially adds or subtracts will run the risk of various related problems. The more evident, and less interesting, is that the resulting text in its compound losses will fall haplessly between two stools: it will neither be a fair rendition of the original poem, nor a good example of the translating poet's own work. As frequently happens with this kind of rendering, a meeting of sensibilities will not have occurred. The second, and more instructive, failure will happen if the "rewriting" translator is acting in anything like good faith as regards the original poem, and not merely colonizing another person's occasion for a display of incompatible mannerisms. This well-meaning adder or subtracter will be manifesting willy-nilly a failure of trust in the expressive characteristics of the poem being imitated. The art of translating poetry rests in making the elements of the original resonate with an equivalent expressive cohesion in the secondary poem. This depends upon a respect for, and a trust in, the original's materials and means. The resulting translation, if felicitous, is also likely to be more respectful of a reader's literary sensibilities.

Luciano Erba's is a poetry of objects. Like other Milanese poets with whom he is associated, he avoids the dangers of high afflatus in the Italian language and its various cultural exploitations by sticking to the details of circumstantial existence. This plain fact is both a creative gift to his translators and a source of necessary communicative difficulty. You could say as much for the fact that his poems are often very short and never particularly extended. The translator has such a small canvas on which to effect an equivalent coordination of parts, and to find a recognizably similar lyrical gesture as that performed by the poem itself. In the translations that follow I have attempted to balance a responsibility to Erba's texts with the need to produce lyrics in English. For those who have some Italian, these translations may be read either as a guide to the *en face* originals, or as one response to the task of translating a poetry that lives in its intimate expressive detail. To those who have little or no Italian, I offer them as faithfully poetic renderings of Erba's verse.

Erba's poetry includes occasional references to social and cultural knowledge with which a reader in another language area cannot be expected to be familiar. Some of this strangeness is, I imagine, what people who enjoy poetry in translation read it for—and it would be unhelpful and misleading to try and naturalize the poems' differences out of existence. So, again in the interests of any particular poem's expressive self-sufficiency, I have attempted to keep notes to a minimum. The author's own notes are translated, with the exception of those that provide information for Italian readers about familiar British and American life and culture. These notes, both the author's and translator's, are given at the back of the book so as to allow those who prefer an unmediated engagement with allusion and difficulty a clean reading text to approach.

I would like to thank Luciano and Mimia Erba for their encouraging support, their help with difficulties in particular passages and references or allusions in the poems, and also for granting permission to publish both the originals and these English versions. My co-translator of Vittorio Sereni, Marcus Perryman, gave valuable advice at an earlier stage of the work. Above all, for her guidance and support with the Italian language, as with everything else in our lives together, I dearly acknowledge my wife Ornella Trevisan.

Peter Robinson
15 November 2005

acknowledgments

Some of these translations or their earlier versions appeared in the following print and electronic publications, to whose editors grateful acknowledgment is made: *Agenda* ("A First-Degree Equation"); *Fire* ("I Live Thirty Meters from the Ground," "End of the Holidays," "One of the Things"); *Kawauchi Review* ("La Grande Jeanne"); *Modern Poetry in Translation* ("La Grande Jeanne," "Tabula Rasa?," "The Mirage," "The Book of Hours," "The Young Couples," "New Methods of Doctor K," "Without Compass," "The Circus Hypothesis," "Railway Suite," "Black Angels," "I Would Like to Enter History"); *Times Literary Supplement* ("The Goodbyes"); *Wandering Dog* ("Graphology of a Goodbye," "A Visit to Caleppio," "Implosion," "The Metaphysical Tramdriver"); *Writing: A Literary Review* ("Far beyond the Frozen Seas"). "Without Reply," "Festival of Nations," "When I Think of My Mother," and "La Vida Es . . ." appeared in Peter Robinson, *The Great Friend and Other Translated Poems* (Tonbridge: Worple Press, 2002); "La Grande Jeanne," "Festival of Nations," "When I Think of My Mother," and "La Vida Es . . ." were anthologized in *The Faber Book of 20th-Century Italian Poems*, edited by Jamie McKendrick (London: Faber & Faber, 2004). A shorter version of the introduction, "The Poetry of Luciano Erba," also appeared in *Modern Poetry in Translation*.

the greener meadow

the poetry of Luciano Erba

The first words of any poem by Luciano Erba that I read were in one by Vittorio Sereni—who had, I later discovered, been his teacher for a year of high school in 1939. "The Alibi and the Benefit," a poem set inside a fog-bound Milanese tram whose doors open onto nothingness, cites lines 1–2 and 4–5 of Erba's early poem "Tabula rasa?": "It's any evening / crossed by half-empty trams" and "You see me advance as you know / in districts without memory?" Sereni sets these as two linked phrases in italics. He leaves out the question mark and adds: "never seen a district so rich in memories / as these so-called 'without' in the young Erba's lines." The young Erba doesn't in fact say that the districts are without memory, he wonders if they are. The difference may seem slight, but is underlined by the different directions taken by the two poems containing these words. In his own 1985 rereading of Sereni's poem, "Mixing Memory and Desire," Erba referred to the quotation of his own early lines as a barrier or obstacle that the poem has to overcome so as to reach its destination. Sereni's goes on to emphasize the fog's ambivalence: it is both a way of avoiding noticing the world's possibilities and the place where they remain with their potentials hidden. His is a poem of self-criticism and tentative cultural optimism.

"The Alibi and the Benefit" was inspired by a moment experienced on Sereni's journey home one evening in 1950. Erba's poem was published in his first collection, *Linea K* (1951):

> It's any evening
> crossed by half-empty trams
> moving to quench their thirst for wind.
> You see me advance as you know
> in districts without memory?
> I've a cream tie, an old
> weight of desires
> I await only the death
> of every thing that had to touch me.

Sereni's comment on the quoted lines serves to indicate the ambivalence about memory half-concealed in Erba's question marks—the ones in the title and at the end of line 5. Is Erba's poem upset by the possibility that the districts may be without memory? Or does the close of his poem reveal that it is inspired by the further desire to see the slate wiped clean? Sereni's poem is set to accuse its poet of being evasive about the roots of the past, of using the fog as his alibi, while simultaneously underlining the hidden benefit in the flourishing of a possible different future. Erba's is poised between the need for a clean start and such a start's potentially alarming emptiness.

Signaling the point of equilibrium between possibilities canvassed by his question marks, there appears, as if a non sequitur, one of Erba's signature details: "I've a cream tie." Italian critics have dwelt upon how often these poems turn to seemingly casual details of wardrobe. Such details too are precisely located between the haphazard and the symbolic, neither one nor the other—as in "La Grande Jeanne," whose desire to rise from poor prostitute to great lady is manifested in her having "a hat already / broad, blue, and with three turns of tulle." The poet's interest in clothes and social ambitions forms part of a much older theme through which settled values are poetically destabilized. The simultaneous fullness and emptiness of our vanities and wishes, revealed by the poems' delicate ironies, is what makes them human. The pathos of unreflected-upon desire and ambition produces instant instances of *carpe diem* and *memento mori*.

Luciano Erba first came to prominence in 1952 when his work was associated with the so-called "Linea Lombarda," thanks to Luciano Anceschi's anthology of that name. Anceschi identified and presented a grouping of poets based in or around Milan with roots in the Luino-Como-Varese "Lake District" of northern Italy. He saw them as sharing a poetry of objects, of understatement, irony, and self-criticism, which included social commentary and cultural commitment—but only if mediated through a skeptical grid of humanistic intelligence and aesthetic detachment. The most senior member of this "line" was Vittorio Sereni (who was among the first to write about his one-time pupil in a 1951 article for *Milano Sera*). Among the other poets anthologized were Erba's contemporary Nelo Risi and Giorgio Orelli. Notwithstanding the reasonable accuracy of this identification, and, what's more, in accord with the assigned characteristics of the group, Erba's short poem "Linea Lombarda" quietly mocks the group's name as yet another commonplace—one that is a little too conveniently true to be more than a misleading pigeonhole.

This helps to explain why his poetry was so largely not to the taste of the postwar neorealists and their theoretically *engagé* successors. In a cultural context where all is "political," detachment of a French nineteenth-century bohemian kind, of a Gautier or Baudelaire, can be crudely construed as reactionary. So Erba, whose poetry is of no convenient party, and who speaks by means of a wry intimacy for the survival of neglected and un-considered ways of life (ones either not yet quite come into existence, or on the way to extinction), has been seen as an apologist for a Catholic conservatism. It's as if he were naturally inclined to side with Giovannino Guareschi's local priest, Don Camillo, in his cold war games of ingenuity and trickery played with the Communist mayor of a village not far from Parma. Yet Erba's approach to the loss-of-faith theme is also distinctly "homemade":

> At waking there comes back the ancient doubt
> if this life weren't a chance event
> and our own just a poor monologue
> of homemade questions and answers.
> I believe, don't believe, when believing I'd like
> to take to the beyond with me a bit of the here
> even the scar that marks my leg
> and keeps me company.

The world and the afterlife are turned inside out. In his later poems, espe-cially, what had seemed a world of solid objects becomes a Cézanne-like mapping of spaces and relations, while the absent and the void is to be furnished with some substance from the here and now. Thus attentive read-ers of these poems will notice that they are no more in thrall to the Catholic Church than they are to a Communist mayor.

Most of Erba's poetry is situated, in one way or another, at points of transit between indeterminate states. These can be geographical, historical, social, political, cultural, and metaphysical. Evident examples in the selec-tion appearing below would be two of the poems from "Railway Suite," which derive from Erba's flight to Switzerland to escape conscription into the forces of Mussolini's Salò Republic, or "The Young Couples," a poem presenting the encounter of a guest and his hosts with their different socio-economic evolutions:

> The young couples of the postwar years
> would lunch in triangular spaces
> of apartments near the fair
> the windows had rings on their curtains
> the furniture was linear, with hardly any books
> the guest who brought Chianti
> we drank from green glass tumblers
> was the first Sicilian I'd ever met
> us, we were his model of development.

What provides this poem with its particular savor is the barely implied mockery of "us," even us, being someone's vision of a better future. Yet it's the presence of just this corrosive perspective that grants pathos to the Sicilian's aspirations. The encounter is decisive for all concerned, but not quite perhaps in the ways they were imagining. Among the many functions of these delicately sketched transitional states is the preservation of a cultural space where the knowledge that poetry is uniquely able to deliver can be brought to life within the course of even so short a poem.

In his editor's introduction to *Poesie 1951–2001*, Stefano Prandi notes that Erba's poems contain the Italian word for "if" 89 times. This word can be used not only to project a space for imaginary possibilities; it may also help maintain an air of skepticism and uncertainty. "The Mirage," for example, flourishes within the vagaries and limits of childhood memory. Such indeterminacy and fluidity of image allow the poetry to do its work independently of those fixities and definites of opinion and ideology that appear to form the unbroken surface of everyday life. Part of Erba's cunning is to achieve his revival of classical epigram by means of a childlike simplicity. Frequently these poems actively promulgate a child's own view of the world, one notoriously subject to the breaking of spells and disillusionment—as in the boys gone fishing in "The Yellow Orris." So the presence of the childlike view keeps the world fresh, while the gentle irony shows it impacted with a more mature knowledge of how things fall out. Similarly, Erba turns history into a kind of child's play. By this means he can contemplate it with detachment and intervene in it ideally. The poet's describing himself as no more than a *chasseur d'images* also points to the seeming paradox that poetry must frequent the apparently insignificant for its sources of fresh meaning. So too, it is only within experiences of the transitorily quotidian that what can stay may be intuited and rendered even as it disappears.

Erba's lifelong skepticism about large systems of thought and explain-all theories appears over the last decade or so to have come into its own. His doubts about psychoanalysis, for example, can be read in the intermittent series of poems concerning Doctor K, the earliest of which dates back half a century or more. Similarly, his apparent portrait of himself as *"petit bourgeois"* in "Without a Compass" subjects various grand designs to a quiet debunking:

> According to Darwin I'd not be of the fittest
> according to Malthus not even born
> according to Lombroso I'll end bad anyway
> and not to mention Marx, me, *petit bourgeois*
> running for it, therefore, running for it
> forward backward sideways
> (as in nineteen-forty when everyone) but
> there remain personal perplexities
> am I to the east of my wound
> or to the south of my death?

The poem outflanks the sorts of class-based political criticism that Erba's work had received at the hands of Franco Fortini and others. Yet, nevertheless, *"petit bourgeois"* is exactly the experience with which Erba's poetry might fictively identify itself, because that is a class in ambivalent transit between two more unequivocally valorized social positions. Something similar could be said for the attribution of essential function to such bit-part players as those from *Hamlet* in "The Circus Hypothesis": "Extras, unmeaning interludes / it's thanks to you perhaps / that the Tightrope walker doesn't fall."

I say "fictively identifies itself" because there has also been a tendency among Italian critics to see Erba's poetry as essentially autobiographical. Again, there is sufficient truth in such a notion for it to be plausible, but not quite enough. After all, there is nothing "confessional" about this poetry, which appears to have few wells of guilt or shame or bad faith to empty out. Here too we can see a difference between his and Sereni's poetry. Erba has said of Fortini's importance in Sereni's life and art that he played the role of a necessary accuser and tormentor. Yet in Erba the autobiography is too close up and too intentionally "inconsequential" to figure as the material of such cultural dramas. Even when he treats of his flight to Switzerland, there is little sense that Erba is narrating an explanatory story that gives shape to his life. He appears rather to be following a vein of reflection or responding to a recurrent impulse. If the mother who makes a number of appearances in these poems appears to be a source of anxiety, the "socialist grandfather" who figures in "Implosion" may be no more nor less than a typical character borrowed, perhaps, from Victor Hugo's *L'Art d'être grand-père*. Similarly, there is no gain in assuming that "The Young Couples" is a poem actually about the poet's life in postwar Milan. It's a representative encounter. For Erba, the minute autobiographical-seeming detail is his quickest means for accessing an experience of life itself.

His work's uniqueness, some might say eccentricity, can be attributed to the poet's being so casually centered upon his own impulse, his own response to the world. It's by no means an unusual condition among distinctively good poets. I'm reminded of Sereni's phrase describing Attilio Bertolucci as a "divino egoista," or that other lake poet Wordsworth's "egotistical sublime." Erba's strategy may have been to seem like a minor epigone of Montale's high cultural snobbism, crossed with a quotidian Milanese adaptation of Jules Laforgue's or Guido Gozzano's irony. But, as P. V. Mengaldo has noted, the epigone's self-proclaimed minor status allows for a wide field of divergence and of camouflaged originality. His work has also been compared to that of a Jacques Prévert—and there is a curious similarity between the informality of means which Erba deploys and that of such Beat poets as Lawrence Ferlinghetti, one of Prévert's most distinguished translators, and just three years older than Erba. Quietly going his own way, borrowing hints for what he has needed from whoever and wherever he likes, while nevertheless sticking to the task of exploring the confines of his own inspiration, Luciano Erba has over more than half a century gone about producing one of the most unusual and original bodies of work in contemporary Italian poetry.

from *Il nastro di Moebius*

The Moebius Strip **(1980)**

Mi sento le guance di cartone
come un ciclista al Giro delle Fiandre
come un tramp nella garitta del frenatore,
coi vetri rotti, tra St. Louis e Detroit
come, gentile lettore, una figura di prua
approfittiamone
è il momento di prendermi a schiaffi.

I feel my cheeks as pasteboard
like a bike rider on the Tour of Flanders
like a tramp in the brakeman's cabin,
with broken panes, between St. Louis and Detroit
like, dear reader, a prow's figurehead
let's take advantage of it
now is the time to slap me in the face.

from *Gradus ad* (Early Poems)

PIOVERÀ

Prima che piova
ripassano le rondini sulla strada.
Passa
un uccello che non conosco
con ala lenta
e volo parallelo alla terra.
La noia
di questo mattino
ritorna al suo cielo di pioggia.

IT WILL RAIN

Before it pours
the swallows pass down the street again.
There passes
a bird I don't recognize
with slow wing
and flight on a level to the earth.
The boredom
of this morning
returns to its skyful of rain.

LA GIACCA A QUADRI

Bon pour la vie
approvò la specchiera
la mia tenuta era perfetta
sorrideva la donna più bella.
Ma tu voce antica
gridasti che era losco
mi parve d'essere cattivo
come non mai
europeo ai tropici
frustare su schiene nude
di portatori
contratti di donne contro oppio
fare e disfare.
Non così, non così
esci di govinezza per sempre
età che ti sfugge
se ieri eri ancora bambino.

THE CHECKED JACKET

Bon pour la vie
the looking-glass approved
my appearance was perfect
the fairest woman smiled.
But ancient voice
it was sinister you cried
to me I seemed nasty
as never before
European in the Tropics
whipping bare backs
of native bearers
contracts in women for opium
to make or to break.
Not like that, not that way
you'll leave youth behind for ever more
age that escapes you
if you were a child still yesterday.

LONTANANZA DA MIA MADRE

Tu anche mi appari agli ultimi sogni
e il giorno per te s'inizia
con altro cielo.
Sul treno delle vacanze
cerco il tuo viso
e le nostre stature
il nostro respiro giovane
oltre i larici.
Mi ridico
per ritrovare la tua voce di allora
certi nomi di luoghi
che pronunciavi indicandoli al di qua della valle.
Amarti è questo, e piangere.
Altro non so. La pena
è certa
è il rimorso.

DISTANCE FROM MY MOTHER

You even appear in the latest dreams
and for you day begins
with a different sky.
On the train for the holidays
I look out for your face
and our heights
our youthful breath
beyond the larches.
To recover your voice of one time
I say again
certain place-names
you would pronounce pointing there across the valley.
This is to love you, and cry.
I know no other. The pain
is certain
it's remorse.

UN'ALTRA CITTÀ

La vignetta del vecchio libro illustrato
sempre sfuggita sotto la velina
per tante volte che lo avevo sfogliato
mi rivela un'altra città
che sale e si distende lungo un fiume
sotto un cielo blu notte.
Dai tetti gli uomini guardano a stelle
che sembrano cervi volanti
appaiono donne ai ballatoi
mentre sull'opposta riva del fiume
un viaggiatore lega a un tronco il cavallo:
ha scoperto anche lui la città.

ANOTHER CITY

The vignette in the old illustrated book
never noticed under its tissue paper
all the times I'd turned the pages
revealed to me another city
that climbs and stretches along a river
under a night-blue sky.
From the roofs men look at stars
which seem like kites
women appear on high loggias
while on the far bank of the river
a traveler ties his horse to a tree-trunk:
he too has discovered the city.

from *Il male minore*

The Lesser Evil (1960)

IL CAVALIERE DEL GARBO

Oppure
svernare agli ultimi piani
nelle cento città. Una corda
molte corde
da una parete all'altra, dai soffitti
al pavimento. Tese.
E il quieto soleggiare sulle dimore.
Mie Rosalbe Carriere
rivedrò i vostri ombrelli piumati?
miei sogni aprirò
le vostre chiuse cerniere?

THE GALLANT GENT

Or else
to winter on the top floors
in a hundred cities. A string
many strings
from one wall to the other, from ceilings
to the floor. Drawn tight.
And the quiet sunshine on the dwellings.
My Rosalba Carrieras
I'll see again your feathered umbrellas?
my dreams will I open
your fastened zips?

NEL PARCO DI VERSAILLES

All'umano mestiere di vivere
pause sub tegmine fagi
quante, o memoria?
A Versailles la carezza di una barca
sul liquido morto del bacino
mi lisciava la pelle.
I bordi, opus Lenotri,
rispondevano in pallide curve
all'eco dei morti paesi
(item un perso biplano
nel decoro di sfatta nuvolaglia).
Così e con voglia di pane
formaggio e fichi
attesi le rane della sera:
io restavo l'ultimo segreto
ma inviolato.

IN THE PARK AT VERSAILLES

To the human business of living
how many pauses
sub tegmine fagi, o memory?
At Versailles a boat's caress
on the basin's dead liquid
was soothing my skin.
The edges, opus Lenotri,
were responding in pale curves
to the echo of dead countries
(item one lost biplane
in the décor of broken cloud cover).
Just so and with a want for bread
cheese and figs
I awaited the evening frogs:
I remained the final secret
but inviolate.

SENTIMENTO DEL TEMPO

a R. G.

Tu mi parli
della traccia di lepre sulla neve
di Mahori cantata dalla radio
quando ti svegli
che danzano a New York.
Ti fidi.
Così se piove sul tetto.
Io non so fermarmi
al segno dell'infinito
in quest'ombra di cose:
la mia pioggia
ha il rumore degli anni.

FEELING OF TIME

for R. G.

You speak to me
of the hare's tracks in snow
of Mahori sung on the radio
when you awake
which they dance to in New York.
You trust.
Do so if it rains on the roof.
I don't know how to remain
at the sign for the infinite
within this shadow of things:
my own rain
has the sound of the years.

UNA STAZIONE CLIMATICA

a Ph. J.

Qui? qui una città dove i cani
corrono coi carretti del latte,
caldo, di giorno e di notte
persone serie nessuna
si tenta la sorte
si mettono nelle fontane
i piedi e le scarpe di tela
si corre lieve sui giorni
senza toccarli nemmeno

dei denari, presto, o mi costituisco.

A HEALTH RESORT

to Ph. J.

Here? here's a town where the dogs
run with the milk carts,
hot, both day and night
serious persons not one
you try fate
feet and canvas shoes
are dipped in the fountains
lightly through the days you run
without even touching them

some money, quick, or I'll turn myself in.

I GLOBULI ROSSI

Per troppi giorni uguali passa un'ora
talvolta calda, forse
come il miglioramento della morte
o la febbre che ammala i petti macri.
La donna costante alla memoria
scende oggi iridata la sua strada
a un battere di ciglia ridestando
i colori del mondo e la follia
che serpeggia i quartieri.
Nel mio cuore
canta questa canzone la passante
piazza dei Vosgi, il dodici settembre.

THE RED GLOBULES

For too many days just the same a sometimes
hot hour passes, perhaps
like the improvement of death
or fever that infects emaciated chests.
The woman constant in memory
goes rainbowed down her street today
in the blink of an eye reawakening
the world's colors and the madness
snaking through the districts.
In my heart
that passerby sings this song
Place des Vosges, the twelfth of September.

SUL TAMIGI

Trascina un'oscura corrente
il fiume, contorna la rocca
di gru degli empori imperiali
di vaniglia e di tè. Noi
gitanti ragazze testimoni
di Jehova avremo bruma sul fiume
stasera, e mugghiar di sirena.
Chi ha infilato il maglione blu mare
dal collo troppo stretto ora riemerge
senza fiato sulla sera fluviale.

ON THE THAMES

An obscure current drags
the river, it surrounds the fortress
of cranes for imperial emporia
of vanilla and tea. We girls
Jehovah's witnesses out on a spree
we'll have mist on the river
this evening, and the foghorn moos.
The one that pulled on a sea-blue sweater
with too tight neck emerges now
out of breath upon the evening's river flow.

GLI IREOS GIALLI

I ragazzi partiti al mattino
di giugno quando l'aria sotto i platani
sembra dentro rinchiudere un'altra aria
i ragazzi partiti alla pesca
con un'unica lenza ma muniti
di un paniere ciascuno a bandoliera
in silenzio ora siedono sul filobus
avviato veloce al capolinea
e il sogno rifanno che Milano
abbia azzurre vallate oltre il Castello
dove saltino i pesci nei torrenti.
Sui prati rimane un po' di nebbia
la tinca nella sua buca di fango
ricomincia a dormire. Mattiniera
la carpa perlustra attorno ai bordi
di un tranquillo canale. La carpa
è astuta e non abbocca mai.
I pescatori non avranno fortuna. Ma
risalendo i canali e le rogge,
di prato in prato, di filare in filare,
arriveranno i ragazzi dove è fitta
la verzura dei fossi, dove gialli
sono i fiori degli ireos e come spade
le foglie tagliano fresche correnti
sotto l'ombra dei salici.
Arriveranno fino ai fiori lontani
i pescatori senza ventura
i ragazzi in gita nella pianura!

THE YELLOW ORRIS

The boys gone one June
morning when air under plane trees
seems to enclose another air
the boys gone fishing
with one rod only but each armed
with a basket slung on shoulders
in silence now sit on the trolley bus
started up fast for the line's end
and they're dreaming again that Milan
has wide blue valleys beyond the Castello
where fish leap in the torrents.
On meadows a bit of fog remains
the tench in its mud hole
goes back to sleep. An early riser
the carp explores around edges
of a tranquil canal. The carp's
cunning and it never takes the bait.
Our fishermen will have no luck. But
climbing canals and culverts upstream
from meadow to meadow, row to row,
the boys will reach where greenery's
thick in the ditches, where orris
flowers are yellow and leaves
cut the fresh currents like swords
under the shadow of willows.
They'll reach right to the distant flowers
those fishermen without good fortune
boys on a trip in the plain!

IL BEL PAESE

Honeste apparenze dei prozii
insediati sul lago! possedere
un panama immenso come il vostro
spostare la torre
sulla scacchiera di legno d'ulivo
e a sera
additare alle donne il Buonaparte
nel profilo del monte!

THE BEAUTIFUL COUNTRY

Honest appearances of great-uncles
located by the lake! to possess
an immense panama hat like yours
to move the castle
on the olivewood chessboard
and with evening
point out to the women
Napoleon in the hill's outline!

LOMBARDO-VENETO

Le donne
al capoluogo scese a servire
in locande di lungofiume
(è un fiume verde scorre tra i sassi
sotto lunghi balconi di legno)
le donne un tempo brave come i preti
nell'andare in cerca di funghi
con passi segreti sulla montagna
ora spolverano i vetri viola e gialli
sulla veranda, le teste di capriolo e
un tavolino da gioco nel vestibolo
sapevano del cielo stellato
stanotte a un abbaiare di cani
all'alba già preparavano il bagno
a un viaggiatore, di legno di castagno
era il fumo entrato nel soppalco
ridevano e che odore di bosco!
Ricordo che ho letto su un giornale
che le donne quaggiù sono le vittime
della rivoluzione industriale.

LOMBARD-VENETO

The women
come down to the local capital
to serve at riverside inns
(it's a green river flows over stones
under long balconies of wood)
the women at one time as good as priests
at going to look for mushrooms
with secret steps on the mountain
now dust yellow and violet panes
on the veranda, a card table
and bucks' heads in the vestibule
they were aware of the starry sky
tonight with a barking of dogs
at dawn were already preparing the bath
for a traveler, the smoke come
into the upper level was of chestnut wood
they were laughing and what a scent of forest!
I remember reading in a newspaper
that the women down here are
industrial revolution victims.

DAL DOTTOR K

(con tre glosse e una variante)

Si sciolga si stenda si rilassi
e associ le immagini del sogno
il sottogola dei preti
la pancia dei tonni
le prugne
le prugne bianche di Boemia[1]
associ! è difficile
ce blanc si tendre de plâtre
sous un ciel de vent d'ouest
sali par les cheminées d'hiver[2]
associ! dopo il viadotto cominciammo a salire
tra due siepi di rovi[3]
associ! salivo scale verniciate di fresco
di case ricominciate
strappavo grumi di minio alle ringhiere
associ, associ! ma ritorna il tonno!
associ si sciolga si rilassi
salivo scale amare sopra il mare
K seduto come Napoleone
decide
salire scale è come (Adler) amare.[4]

---

[1] eravamo partiti da Mariahilfe
  fino ai fiori dei fagioli
  tra i papaveri d'alta montagna
[2] *Variante*
  ce blanc des cuisses des filles
  quand elles quittent leurs bas noirs dans un meublé
[3] fu un'estate di fiori divelti
  di treni freschi, d'imposte socchiuse
[4] fu quando su una sedia di vimini
  tatuavo la scema di Rimini?

WITH DOCTOR K

(with three glosses and a variant)

Loosen up stretch out relax
and associate dream images
the priests' dog collars
tuna fishes' bellies
the plums
white plums from Bohemia[1]
associate! it's difficult
ce blanc si tendre de plâtre
sous un ciel de vent d'ouest
sali par les cheminées d'hiver[2]
associate! after the viaduct we started to climb
between two blackberry hedges[3]
associate! I was climbing up just varnished stairs
of houses in reconstruction
I was tearing flakes of red from balustrades
associate, associate! but the tuna comes back!
associate loosen up relax
I was climbing bitter stairs high above
the sea, K sitting like Napoleon
decides
to climb stairs is like (Adler) to love.[4]

[1] we had gone from Mariahilfe
   as far as the bean flowers
   among high mountain poppies
[2] *Variant*
   ce blanc des cuisses des filles
   quand elles quittent leurs bas noirs dans un meublé
[3] it was a summer of uprooted flowers
   of airy trains, of shutters half-closed
[4] was it when in a wickerwork chair
   I tattooed the idiot Rimini woman?

UNDECIDED

In mezzo al deserto ho un tappeto
ho due donne trovate in Europa
era tempo scoprissi il segreto
si chiama ama e gioca.
A sera raccolgo le dita
di Perduta lunghe infinite
e di Nera che viene d'Irlanda
e che sanno lavare.
Ma di giorno
veleggiamo in cima dei cotogni
e stacchiamo le pietre sui pendii.

UNDECIDED

In the middle of the desert I've a carpet
I've two women found in Europe
it was time I learned the secret
they call love and play.
Evenings I gather up the fingers
of Perduta infinitely long
and of Nera who's from Ireland
and which know how to wash.
But through the day
we sail atop the quince trees
and knock stones off the cliffs.

SENZA RISPOSTA

Ti ha portata novembre. Quanti mesi
dell'anno durerà la dolceamara
vicenda di due sguardi, di due voci?
Se io avessi una leggenda tutta scritta
direi che questo tempo che ci sfiora
ci appartiene da sempre. Ma non sono
che un uomo tra mille e centomila
ma non sei
che una donna portata da novembre
e un mese dona e un altro ci saccheggia.
Sei una donna
che oggi tiene un naufrago impaziente
dimmi tu
sei scoglio
o continente?

WITHOUT REPLY ✓

November has brought you. How many months
of the year will the bitter-sweet
affair of two looks, of two voices endure?
If I had a tale entirely written
this time brushing past us I would say
has always been ours. But I'm only
a man among thousands and hundreds of thousands
but you're only
a woman that November brings
and one month grants and another plunders from us.
You're a woman
who's holding today an impatient
castaway, then tell me
are you rock
or continent?

LA GRANDE JEANNE

La Grande Jeanne non faceva distinzioni
tra inglesi e francesi
purché avessero le mani fatte
come diceva lei
abitava il porto, suo fratello
lavorava con me
nel 1943.
Quando mi vide a Losanna
dove passavo in abito estivo
disse che io potevo salvarla
e che il suo mondo era lì, nelle mie mani
e nei miei denti che avevano mangiato lepre in alta montagna.

In fondo
avrebbe voluto la Grande Jeanne
diventare una signora per bene
aveva già un cappello
blu, largo, e con tre giri di tulle.

LA GRANDE JEANNE ✓

It made no difference to la Grande Jeanne
whether they were English or French
so long as they had hands
the way she liked them
she lived by the port, her brother
was working with me
in 1943.
When she met me at Lausanne
where I would stop in summer clothes
she told me I could save her
and that her world was there, in my hands
and my teeth which had eaten hare in high mountains.

At heart
la Grande Jeanne would have liked
to become a respectable lady
she had a hat already
broad, blue, and with three turns of tulle.

DON GIOVANNI

La Nene ha un gran cappello
a sesti di piqué
e colorati sopra
lamponi e raisinet.
Per me è un gran gelato
servito con la frutta
ma non si dica a Nene
che nel mese di agosto
le starò sempre accanto
per quel cappello bianco.

DON JUAN

Miss Nene has a great hat
in segments of piqué
and colored on top
strawberries and red currants.
To me it's a great
ice cream served with fruit
but don't say to Nene
that in the month of August
I'll always be close by her
because of that white hat.

UN'EQUAZIONE DI PRIMO GRADO

La tua camicetta nuova, Mercedes
di cotone mercerizzato
ha il respiro dei grandi magazzini
dove ci equipaggiavano di bianchi
larghissimi cappelli per il mare
cara provvista di ombra! per attendervi
in stazioni fiorite di petunie
padri biancovestiti! per amarvi
sulle strade ferrate fiori affranti
dolcemente dai merci decollati!
E domani, Mercedes
sfogliare pagine del tempo perduto
tra meringhe e sorbetti al Biffi Scala.

A FIRST-DEGREE EQUATION

Your latest blouse, Mercedes
of mercerized cotton
has the fresh air of department stores
where they kit us out for the sea
with broadest-brimmed white hats
dear provisioned shade! to wait
in stations decked with petunias
for fathers clothed in white! to love you
broken-hearted flowers on the lines
gently cut off by freight trains!
And tomorrow, Mercedes
to leaf over pages of *temps perdu*
at the Biffi Scala amongst sorbets and meringues.

TERRA E MARE

Goletta, gentilissimo legno, svelto
prodigio! se il cuore
sapesse veleggiare come sai
tra gli azzurri arcipelaghi!

ma tornerò alla casa sulla rada
verso le sei, quando la Lenormant
avanza una poltrona sul terrazzo
e si accinge ai lavori di ricamo
per le mense d'altare.

Navigazione blu, estivi giorni
sere dietro una tenda a larghe maglie
come una rete! bottiglie
vascelli tra rocchi di conchiglie
e la lettura di Giordano Bruno
nel salotto di giunco, nominatim
De la Causa Principio e Uno!

LAND AND SEA

Schooner, tenderest vessel, slim
prodigy! if only the heart
knew how to sail as you do
through blue archipelagoes!

but I'll return to the house on the roadstead
towards six, when Madame Lenormant
draws up an armchair on the terrace
and sets about her needlework
for the altar tables.

Blue sailing, summer days
evenings behind a broad-stitched curtain
like a net! ships in bottles
among seashell rocks
and the reading of Giordano Bruno
in the wicker sitting room, nominatim
Of the First Cause and the One!

QUALCOSA

È una via di Milano
e veloce
vado verso l'oriente.
Già si vedono delle luci
ma il cielo è ancora chiaro
chiare le nuvole lontane.
Tra poco svolterò
per tornare ai miei libri
raccolto
nel loro segreto
e a notte
sarò dietro le imposte
come una statua ansiosa.

SOMETHING ✓

It's a Milanese street
and I'm heading fast
towards the east.
Already you see some lights
but the sky's still clear
clear the distant clouds.
Soon I'll turn round
to go back to my books
gathered up
in their secret
and at night
I will be behind shutters
like a nervous statue.

TABULA RASA?

È sera qualunque
traversata da tram semivuoti
in corsa a dissetarsi di vento.
Mi vedi avanzare come sai
nei quartieri senza ricordo?
Ho una cravatta crema, un vecchio peso
di desideri
attendo solo la morte
di ogni cosa che doveva toccarmi.

TABULA RASA?

It's any evening
crossed by half-empty trams
moving to quench their thirst for wind.
You see me advance as you know
in districts without memory?
I've a cream tie, an old
weight of desires
I await only the death
of every thing that had to touch me.

IL MIRAGGIO

Un pozzo sembrava
quel cerchio di bianche pietre
sottomarine.
Mio fratello lasciò i remi
anch'io guardavo dal sandolino.
Una volta
prima che il mare salisse
attingevano a questo pozzo.
Ma era salito il mare?
Forse un gioco d'arenarie
o un anello di scogli
stava sul fondo sabbioso. Oppure
un ordinato naufragare di pietre
zavorra di antichi naviganti.
Inavvertite correnti ci mossero.
Ora sul fondo
mi confondeva
una lenta danza di alghe. Cercavamo
non v'erano che ciuffi verdastri
sul fondo a trasparire.
Dal remo fredde gocce d'acqua
caddero a abbrividirmi.
Freddo vento ci avvertì della sera.

THE MIRAGE

It seemed like a well
that circle of white stones
underneath the waves.
My brother let go of the oars
I too looked from the rowboat.
At some point
before the sea rose
they drew from this well.
But had the sea risen?
Perhaps it was a sandstone puzzle
or a ring of rocks
was on the sandy bottom. Or else
a tidy-looking wreck of stones
ancient sailors' ballast.
Unnoticed currents moved us.
On the bottom now
a slow dance of algae
confused me. We were searching
there were only greenish tufts
grown visible on the bottom.
From the oar cold drops of water
fell to give me shivers.
Cold wind made us notice the evening.

LIBRO D'ORE

Come dice il poeta delle Ande
chi le nubi non ama
non venga non venga all'Ecuador.
E non entri di marzo nel pometo
dove avventa garbino scatenato
sull'acerba verzura. Oggi
tumultuano scalmane di velieri
nell'azzurro di Francia. Ed è
tempo nuovo dell'anno
che incontra il nostro cammino
un'aspra follia equinoziale
per slogare caviglie e spiritare
queste sagge quinconce.
Stanchi sogniamo
di verdi ferrovie lillipuziane
dentro e fuori dei picchi a pan di zucchero.
In città ci lasciamo
tra quarzo e mica di costruzioni
gela la primaluna, noi rientriamo
inseguiti dappresso dalla vita
come da un cane amico che ci raggiunga.

BOOK OF HOURS

As the poet of the Andes says
those who don't love clouds
don't come don't come to Ecuador.
And in March don't enter the orchard
where an unleashed southwest wind
rips at the raw greenery. Today
agitations of sailing ships riot
in the azure of France. And it's
the year's springtime
that meets our hike
a sour equinoctial folly
to dislocate ankles and craze
these wise quincunxes.
Tired we dream
of green lilliputian railways
inside and out of the sugarloaf peaks.
In the city we separate
amid building-site quartz and mica
the new moon freezes, we return home
pursued at our heels by life
as by a friendly dog that catches up with us.

CAINO E LE SPINE

Era mattina, erano le tre
quell'aria non aveva coscienza.
Ti offrivi al primo fresco e
perché? cani da guardia, ore, perché?
perché te stesso?
La ghiaia in strada si faceva chiara
la fontana rideva tra i bossi
intorno erano cose molto femmine
disinvolte ad esistere.
Passavi il filo spinato
senza scarpe rientravi al convento.

CAIN AND THE THORNS

It was morning, it was three o'clock
that air did not have consciousness.
You offered yourself to the first cool breeze
and why? guard dogs, hours, why?
why you yourself?
The gravel on the road was growing clear
the fountain was giggling among box trees
all around were things very feminine
self-confidently existing.
You were crossing the thorny line
without shoes were re-entering the convent.

DIGNUS EST INTRARE

Quanto buio tra i campi di zucche
quanti colli d'ogni pianura!
Alato addio
non s'impigli il tuo volo alle robinie
torna dove una bianca lontananza
già annuncia oltre il monte le tue schiere
torna e raccolte l'ali, del viaggio
racconta sulle sponde del mio carro
guidato con freschissime mani
racconta i fantasmi dei villaggi
come panni agitati dal vento
e la notte d'agosto quale lebbra
bianca che rode strade e cascinali
i campi d'avena racconta
i campi di stelle
e le mie guance nuove se le sfebbra
pallido un pagliaio!

DIGNUS EST INTRARE

So much dark across the pumpkin fields
so many hills for every plain!
Winged god-be-with-you
don't tangle your flight in robinias
come back where a white distance
already announces your hosts beyond the mountain
come back and, wings gathered, recount
your journey on my wagon's sides
guided by the freshest hands
recount village specters
like laundry disturbed by the wind
and the August night like white
leprosy gnawing at roads and farmsteads
recounts the oat fields
the fields of stars
and my renewed cheeks should a pale
haystack cool their fever!

IPPOGRAMMI & METAIPPOGRAMMI
DEL PITTORE GIOVANOLA

. . . d'improvviso questi cavalli sono un'altra cosa
io non dico giraffe bisonti uomini tori formicole
né cavalli di pezza lasciati malconci da un bimbo
né cavalli di panno riempiti da quattro pagliacci
resteremmo in un campo di pure associazioni d'idee
se fosse solo così. Dico invece che questi cavalli
selvaggi o anche ammaestrati
ma raramente domi, e comunque per loro volontà
che questi bradi o sapienti, ma per quanto sopra autodidatti cavalli
recalcitranti il più delle volte,
riottosi, in fuga dal foglio di carta
o cheti a quel loro modo un po' subdolo
e pateticamente allora pensosi
della madre steppa ovunque annusata
ovvero (e per mano di aiuti del colonnello Stumpfmayer:
di origine italiana? e potrà eseguire domani
il suo numero danzante davanti all'Imperatore?)
confitti, rivenduti al teatro d'anatomia, colà alfine arresi
che questi cavalli
(accade non so dove in oriente
che a monaci e arcieri si rivelino
mondi nuovissimi
per una freccia trent'anni lanciata
allo stesso bersaglio
per una preghiera detta e ridetta
su interminabili rosari di osso,
non accade a noi forse per un volto
conosciuto ma sin qui indifferente
di trovarci ad un tratto ad amare?)

HIPPOGRAMS & METAHIPPOGRAMS
OF THE PAINTER GIOVANOLA

. . . of a sudden these horses are something else
I don't say giraffes bison men bulls tiny ants
nor rag horses left in shreds by a child
nor clothes horses heaped up by four clowns
we'd remain in a field of pure associations of ideas
if it were only thus. Rather I say these horses
savage or trained too
but rarely tamed, and in any case by their own will
that these wild or wise, but for those above self-taught horses
recalcitrant most times,
rioting, in flight from the sheet of paper
or quiet in their way a bit shifty
and then pathetically pensive
about the mother steppes they sniff everywhere
that's to say (and by means of help from colonel Stumpfmayer:
of Italian descent? and will he be able tomorrow to perform
his dance number in front of the Emperor?)
pinned down, sold back to the anatomy theatre, giving in there at last . . .
that these horses
(it happens I don't know where in the orient
that to monks and archers are revealed
the newest worlds
by an arrow sent for thirty years
at the same target
for a prayer said and repeated
over interminable rosaries of bone,
doesn't it happen to us for a known face
but till now indifferent
to find ourselves suddenly loving?)

che per questi cavalli
a pezzi interi sdraiati
accoppiati soli e d'un tratto
più di là che di qua
Giovanola ha varcato i confini
di una terra di uomini longilinei
brachicefali, esperti di metalli
dell'arco e di un tipo di lotta
ben diversa da quella delle Ryu-Kyu.
Nessuno può dire se i cavalieri
immobili in sella ai cavalli
vengano dal mare o dall'altopiano
oppure da un continente sommerso
né quando il loro momento sia stato
né se debba ancora arrivare.
Occorreranno altri cavalli
per saperne qualcosa di più.
Siamo adesso alla fondazione di un alfabeto
se i cavalli vorranno, se i cavalli . . .

that for these horses
in pieces entire reclining
paired alone and suddenly
more gone beyond than in the here and now
Giovanola's crossed over the confines
of a land of elongated
brachycephalic men, experts in metals
in the bow and a kind of wrestling
very different from that of the Ryukyu.
No one can say if the riders
motionless on their horses' saddles
come from the sea or the high plateau
or else from a sunken continent
nor when their moment had been
nor if it has still to arrive.
Other horses will be required
to learn something more of it.
We're now at the founding of an alphabet
if the horses want it, if the horses . . .

NELLA TORRE D'AVORIO

Vorrei rileggere
le avventure del soldatino di stagno, o
narrare lunghe storie di cose
che dobbiamo lasciare. Lontani
destini di cose: in aeternum.
Come palloni sciabole frustini
o animali, dico pappagalli
(in terrazzo avevamo un'uccelliera
mi appoggiavo a guardare, un po' di ruggine
restava sulla fronte) o il più grande coniglio
che avevo accarezzato in piazza d'armi
qualche piuma che avrebbe potuto cadere
ai bersaglieri in corsa nei viali.

Narrare e descrivere: medaglie
nuvole cieli tappezzerie
cifre che nascono ai capelli
lamed zain aleph
a D nei mattini di giugno.

IN THE IVORY TOWER ✓

I'd like to reread
the little tin soldier's adventures, or
tell long stories of things
we've to leave behind. Remote
destinies of things: in aeternum.
Like balloons sabers whips
or animals, let's say parrots
(an aviary we had on the terrace
I leaned there to look, a little rust
remained on my forehead) or the largest
rabbit I'd stroked on the parade ground
some feathers that could have fallen
from bersaglieri running down the avenues.

To tell and describe: medals
clouds tapestries skies
ciphers that are born in the hair
lamed zayin aleph
to D on June mornings.

VANITAS VARIETATUM

Io talvolta mi chiedo
se la terra è la terra
e se queste tra i viali del parco
sono proprio le madri.
Perché passano una mano guantata
sul dorso di cani fedeli?
perché bambini scozzesi
spiano dietro gli alberi
qualcuno, scolaro o soldato
che ora apre un cartoccio
di torrone o di zucchero filato?
Ottobre è rosso e scende dai monti
di villa in villa
e di castagno in castagno
si stringe ai mantelli
accarezza il tricolore sul bungalow
nel giorno che i bersaglieri
entrano ancora a Trieste.
Tutto è dunque morbido sotto gli alberi
presso le madri e i loro mantelli aranciati
la terra, la terra e ogni pena d'amore
esiste altra pena?
sono di là dai cancelli: così le Furie
e le opere non finite.

Ma queste non sono le madri
io lo so, sono i cervi in attesa.

VANITAS VARIETATUM ✓

I sometimes ask myself
if the earth's the earth
and if these ones between park avenues
are actually the mothers.
Why do they pass a gloved hand
along the backs of faithful dogs?
Why do Scots children
spy behind trees
someone, schoolboy or soldier
opening a paper cone
of nougat or cotton candy now?
October is red and comes down
the hillsides from villa to villa
and chestnut to chestnut
it presses on the capes
caresses the tricolore above the bungalow
on the day the bersaglieri
once more enter Trieste.
So everything's soft beneath the trees
near the mothers and their orange capes
the earth, the earth and every pain of love
does other pain exist?
they're beyond the gates: just so the Furies
and the unfinished works.

But these aren't the mothers
I know, they're deer waiting.

MOLTO DI LÀ DAGLI AGGHIACCIATI MARI

Conosco una città
diceva nel breve cerchio di luce
di un falò la guida diplomata
con un ponte lunghissimo di ferro
gettato su un quartiere popolare
ricordo dei caffè prima del ponte
i grandi magazzini un teatrino
sintetico o sovietico sono vecchio
e non so bene, una vera città
di donne col cappello a cilindro
oppure con le scarpe chiodate
sarà più semplice entrare dal camino
dicevano sul ponte con un soffio
e un breve cenno alle case di sotto
le stanze . . .
Gli scienziati accampati sulla ghiaia
in silenzio ascoltavano la guida
ma nessuno chiedeva a quanti giorni
di cavallo distasse la città.
Si mise a camminare in su e in giù:
stanze più lunghe che larghe
giacinti alle doppie finestre
giardini di fragole e lattuga
in cucina riflessi di fuoco
al tramonto, piastrelle . . . La missione
della reale società geografica
era vinta dal sonno. Piastrelle
ormai la guida parlava alle stelle.

FAR BEYOND THE FROZEN SEAS ✓

I know a city
in the bonfire's small circle of light
the qualified guide was saying
with a quite long iron bridge
thrown over a modest district
cafés I recall before the bridge
the large stores a little theatre
synthetic or soviet I'm old
and don't know well, a real city
of women with top hats
or else with hobnailed shoes
it'll be easier to enter by the chimney
they said on the bridge with a whisper
and a brief wave at houses below
at the rooms . . .
The scientists encamped on the gravel
were listening in silence to the guide
but nobody asking how many days
away on horseback was the city.
He started to walk up and down:
rooms much longer than wide
hyacinths at double windows
gardens with lettuce and strawberries
reflections of fire in the kitchen
at sunset, tiled walls . . . The mission
from the royal geographical society
was defeated by sleep. Tiled walls
by now the guide was speaking to the stars.

LO SVAGATO

Ma quando arrivano? e come?
e chi li manda tra noi?
un giorno li trovi vicini
con un berretto a visiera
la sciarpa rossa, le mani
nelle tasche davanti dei calzoni
nuovi compagni dei nostri giochi
silenziosi, sorridenti compagni
più piccoli di noi, più pallidi
stanchi a una breve corsa, maldestri
a lottare, a saltare, e senza peso.
Ricordo uno che un mattino d'ottobre
salì con noi fino al monte Cavallo
aveva le guance rosse di mal di cuore
sorrideva correndo per restarci vicino.
E un altro, né escludo che fosse lo stesso
per quel loro modo di camminare e il maglione turchino,
che per vigneti mi seguì al fondovalle
a pesca di trote dove il fiume
si dirama in chiari canali.
Si restò fino a sera dentro l'acqua
senza che mi chiedesse una volta
di provare a pescare: poi scomparve
per un sentiero che non saprei più trovare.
E un terzo, o ancora lo stesso,
per quel loro grande nodo alla sciarpa di lana,
e per il suo starmi in silenzio vicino
nei prati gialli fuori città
in un'Africa immaginata
per un'immobile, lunga giornata. E un quarto . . .

THE INATTENTIVE

But when do they arrive? and how?
and who sends them among us?
one day you find them near
with a peaked cap
red scarf, hands
in trouser front pockets
new companions for our games
silent, smiling companions
smaller, paler than us
tired from a short race, clumsy
at wrestling, jumping, weightless.
I recall one who an October morning
climbed with us far as Monte Cavallo
he had red cheeks from heart disease
he smiled as he ran to stay near us.
And another, or the same one, I can't rule it out,
from their way of walking and the loud blue sweater,
who followed me through vineyards to the valley floor
to fish for trout where the river
branches out into bright channels.
We stayed till evening in the water
without him asking me even one time
for a try of the rod: then he vanished
down a path that I wouldn't ever find.
And a third, or the same again,
from the big knot in their woolen scarf,
and from his standing in silence by me
in the yellow fields beyond the city
in an imagined Africa
for a long, still day. And a fourth . . .

Scomparsi. Distrutti da febbri spietate,
consunti da un male ignoto, lontani, non so.
Né so se torneranno, né quando, né come
gli amici, i giorni, la più chiara stagione,
se tornerà la vita
perduta per disattenzione.

Disappeared. Destroyed by ruthless fevers
consumed by an unknown ill, far off, I don't know.
Nor do I know if they'll return, nor when, nor how
the friends, the days, the brighter season,
if it will return, life
that's lost through inattention.

INCOMPATIBILITÀ

Sin tanto che don Oldani
e i venticinque esploratori
si rincorrono su queste lastre di piombo
io mi immagino il popolo di donne
della cerchia più antica della città.
Addormentate agli ultimi piani
in un letto di ferro
quante sognano la mia sciarpa di seta?
Guardo la città grigiorossa
domenicale, dal terrazzo del duomo
ma potessi volare
ai bei gerani sulle lunghe ringhiere
varcare porte, a piedi nudi
camminare sugli esagoni rossi
poi vedermi alle vostre specchiere
brune ninette, che abitate il verziere!
Partono adesso i crociati
io rimango quassù
con una spia albanese
che fotografa torri e ciminiere.

INCOMPATIBILITY ✓

For as long as Don Oldani
and the twenty-five boy scouts
chase each other on these sheets of lead
I muse on the women populace
from the city's oldest circle.
Fallen asleep on top floors
in a bed of iron
how many dream about my silk scarf?
I look at the reddish-gray city
of a Sunday, from the cathedral terrace
but could I fly
to the lovely geraniums on the long balustrades
pass through doors, with naked feet
walk on the red hexagonals
then see myself in your mirrors
brown-haired ninettes who live by the market!
Now the crusaders depart
I remain high above here
with an Albanian spy
who photographs towers and chimneys.

SUPER FLUMINA

Vedrò gli anni, i visi, i paesi
in cerchio, a passo di danza
se mai avrò una giacca di velluto
qualche pipa di schiuma
il vino rosso d'una mia terra.
Se avrò una torre e le mele nei cassetti.

Quel giorno sarò un amico del popolo.
Ma oggi è tempo di necessarie triangolazioni.

Per una gita sul fiume, domenicale
partiamo: e distanziati i sobborghi
si risale tutto un piano inclinato
di strade e campagne rannuvolate
si pone il piede sui primi termini alti
aggirati da una fiumana impetuosa
che fa a pezzi la roccia, la travolge
o la scheggia e incenerisce alle anse.

Le nuotatrici in secco sul ghiaione
hanno costumi a fiori, esuli coppie
vanno e vengono per più interne rovine
tra i pruni sbiancati e senza frutti.
Una barca fa acqua, le sorelle
continuano a vuotarla, ma il traghetto
resta sempre di qua. Vi è la scalata
di un generoso sul nudo ciglione
lo attardano un paniere di merenda
e la compagna dai sandali d'oro
un'altra vana impresa se fra i rovi
spunta lui solo, sogguarda, se ne va.

SUPER FLUMINA

I'll see the years, faces, lands
in a circle, dancing
if ever I have a velvet coat
some meerschaum pipes
the red wine from my own land.
If I've a tower and apples in trays.

That day I'll be the people's friend.
But today's a time of necessary triangulations.

For an outing on the river one Sunday
we leave: and suburbs in the distance
we climb up an inclined plane
of roads and clouded-over fields,
set a foot on the first high boundaries
encircled by an impetuous flood
which breaks rock in pieces, tumbles
or splinters and burns it to dust on the turns.

The swimmer-girls high and dry on the gravel
have flowery costumes, exiled couples
come and go through more inner ruins
among whitened thorns with no fruit.
A boat lets in water, the sisters
continue to bail, but the ferry
stays forever over here. There's the climb
up the bare bank of a kind one
slowed down by a snack basket
and his gold-sandaled companion
another vain endeavor if through brambles
only he emerges, glances, goes away.

Vorrei non ritentasse, che la barca
delle controdanaidi ripartisse
e che all'ombra dentata della draga
non più giacesse un affranto Issione.
Vorrei non fossero tartarei supplizi
sulle rive dell'Adda, il dì festivo
ma questo è un tempo d'inevitabili triangolazioni.

Ecco s'alza dal fondo, in bigie piume
un che non è re di quaglia o pernice.
Ha l'ali troppo lente, il volo sazio
d'antichissimo sangue: e così vola
oltre la groppa d'ogni calva collina.
Già i tre cacciatori cinesi
hanno alzato i lunghi fucili
ma nessuno che sappia
che l'ignoranza è il male minore
presso i fedeli dell'imperatore?

I'd rather he didn't try again, so
the counter-Danaides' boat would leave again
and in the dredge's toothed shadow
would no longer lie a broken Ixion.
I'd rather there weren't tarter torments
on the banks of the Adda, a feast day
but this is a time of unavoidable triangulations.

Look there rises from the deep, in gray feathers
one who's not king of quail or partridge.
Its wings are tardy, the flight filled full
of the most ancient blood: and so it flies
beyond the backs of each bald hill.
Already the three Chinese hunters
have raised their long rifles
but no one who understands
that ignorance is the lesser evil
among those faithful to the emperor?

AEROSTATICA

Ricordi quel pomeriggio di giugno
Zunette dalla terrazza di B
improvvisa diruppe la pioggia
mentre nel cielo di piombo
fioriva la mongolfiera del comandante Gérard.
Non era comandante Gérard
e col suo maglione *à double face*
si prendeva dei gran raffreddori
diceva: sternuto sempre tre volte di fila.
Non aveva equipaggio Gérard
era un uomo, che si staccava da terra.
Ma un giorno t'invitò a salire in pallone
tu sventolavi tra cielo e terra
ricordi, il tuo cappello di paglia
col nastro rosso da gondoliere.
Non vi ho più rivisti.

AEROSTATICS ∿

You remember that June afternoon
Zunette from B's terrace
unexpected the rain poured down
while the leaden sky blossomed
with commander Gérard's hot air balloon.
He wasn't a commander Gérard
and with his jersey *à double face*
he would catch terrible colds
he'd say: I always sneezed three times in a row.
He didn't have a crew Gérard
was a man, who'd detach from the earth.
But one day he invited you to ascend in his balloon
you were fluttering between earth and sky
remember, your straw hat
with red ribbon like a gondolier.
I never saw you again.

DOPO LE VACANZE

La tua camicetta bianca, Carlina,
chi l'ha stirata con tanta cura?
non era meglio stirato né più fresco
il fazzoletto che a scuola
si restituiva al compagno di banco
se il giorno prima avevamo avuto sangue da naso.
Sei tu la gentile stiratrice?
è già autunno, Carlina,
questo maggio d'autunno che è settembre
ed è tempo
di rimettere A maiuscola all'amore.

AFTER THE HOLIDAYS ✓

Your white blouse, Carlina,
who ironed it with such care?
The handkerchief at school
given back to the classmate
if we'd had a bloody nose the day before
was no less fresh nor better ironed.
The tender ironer, is it you?
it's already autumn, Carlina,
this autumn's May which is September
and it's time
to put the capital L back into love.

from *Il prato più verde*

The Greener Meadow (1977)

GLI ANNI QUARANTA

Sembrava tutto possibile
lasciarsi dietro le curve
con un supremo colpo di freno
galoppare in piedi sulla sella
altre superbe cose
più nobili prospere cose
apparivano all'altezza degli occhi.
Ora gli anni volgono veloci
per cieli senza presagi
ti svegli da azzurre trapunte
in una stanza di mobili a specchiera
studi le coincidenze dei treni
passi una soglia fiorita di salvia rossa
leggi «Salve» sullo zerbino
poi esci in maniche di camicia
ad agitare l'insalata nel tovagliolo.
La linea della vita
deriva tace s'impunta
scavalca sfila
tra i pallidi monti degli dei.

MY FORTIES

It all seemed possible
leaving the curves behind
with definitive squeal of brakes
galloping off stood on the saddle
other lofty things
more noble prosperous things
were appearing at eye level.
Now the years turn quickly
in skies without omens
you awake from blue quilts
to a room with mirrored furniture
study the train connections
cross a threshold blossoming with red sage
read "Welcome" on the mat
then go out in shirt sleeves
to shake the salad in a napkin.
The Life Line drifts
keeps silent won't shift
it hurdles it passes
between the pale hills of the gods.

TRA SPAZIO E TEMPO

Per kelle fini
abbiamo perso anche il kappa
la nevosa cortina delle alpi dunque
ma-con-gran-pena comunque
salivamo le mulattiere del re
salivamo ogni monte più alto
mondo del mattino
mattino del mondo
Le Monde! Le Matin!
la guerra era nell'aria
le gente si divertiva
poi qualcuno ha fatto strada
e in soprabito e cappello
comanda uomini tutti uguali.

BETWEEN SPACE AND TIME

"Per kelle fini"
we've even lost the K
the snowy curtain of the alps then
maybe-costing-great-pain anyway
we were climbing the mule tracks of the king
we were climbing every higher mountain
world of the morning
morning of the world
Le Monde! Le Matin!
the war was in the air
the people were entertained
then someone got ahead
and dressed to the nines
he commands men all the same.

HALLOWEEN

Dietro un banco di birra
ho ritrovato l'archetipo
ho rivisto i miei anni di cimbro
in doppiopetto marrone
pelle più liscia, meno liscia
confuso e avveduto, fedele.
Quando esco nella campagna collinare
le zucche dove ardono i lumi
hanno figura di teschio
è la vigilia dei Santi
i piccoli sono in festa
i cimbri affondano nella nebbia.

HALLOWEEN

Behind a bar of beer
I've rediscovered the archetype
I've seen again my cymbric years
in brown double-breasted
skin smoother, less smooth
confused and wary, faithful.
When I go out in hill country
the pumpkins where lights burn
have the shape of a skull
it's the night before All Saints
the little ones are in high spirits
in fog the cymbrians drown.

EPIFANIA

C'è in questo cielo di gennaio
della dodicesima notte
un'infinita pazienza
non nascono domande
non occorre alzare gli occhi allo zenith
e non fa differenza seguire
la linea dei camini sui tetti
o lungo il granito dei muri
vedere, non vedere
tanto passare di umane ombre nere.

EPIPHANY ✓

There is in this January sky
on twelfth night
an infinite patience
no questions have their birth
no need to lift eyes towards the zenith
and it makes no difference whether you follow
the line of chimneys on the roofs
or along the granite of walls
to see, or not to see
such a passing of black human shadows.

TRASFERIMENTO

Tetti si appoggiano a tetti
ti abitui alla nuova città
discendono calde trapunte
dai balconi nel sole invernale
esci con scarpe marrone
lucide come castagne d'india
ma a sera quando viene la nebbia
e la gente si ritrova nei bar
fra alzate di bottiglie e di pandori
tu punti all'azzurra insegna nebbiosa
di un'esposizione di mobilia
dove guardi i letti damascati
le pettineuses i buffé i contrabuffé
poi rientri e stai a lungo allo specchio.

RELOCATION

Roofs abut on roofs
you get used to the new city
warm counterpanes hang
from the balconies in winter sun
you go out in brown shoes
shining like Indian chestnuts
but with evening when fog comes
and people meet up in bars
amid shelves of bottles and pandoro cakes
you head for the foggy blue sign
of a furniture shop display
where you look at the damask beds
the pettineuses the buffé the contrabuffé
then go home and stand a long time at the mirror.

BARCELLONA BALTIMORA...

a Lucia

Operose città di cielo rosa
d'alti cespi alte case alte terrazze
sovrapposti habitat e spalle di giganti
tra voi non occorrono orologi
né meridiane, rousseau, trovate di giovani esploratori
per accorgersi delle dieci di mattina
nei giorni che vengono prima
che vengono dopo
le grandi vacanze d'estate
un trillo di ciclista annuncia l'ora
nel pulviscolo aurato
oppure un tocco di martello
da profondi cortili
o il dirigibile che con lievi matite
disegna sull'album raffaello
la mia figlia più bionda.

BARCELONA BALTIMORE ... ✓

to Lucia

Industrious cities with rose skies
high shrubs high houses high balconies
superimposed habitats and giants' shoulders
no need of clocks among you
nor meridians, rousseau, boy scouts' discoveries
to realize it's ten in the morning
in the days that come earlier
that come later
the great summer holidays
a cyclist's bell marks the time
in the golden dust
or else the hammer's ring does
from within deep courtyards
or the airship drawn with faint pencil
on the raphael album
by my blondest daughter.

PASTELLO

alle piccole
Francesca e Caterina

ma come può un coniglio
fare il prato più verde
una strada ferrata
una stazione di mattoni rossi
nascondersi fra colline di robinie
per farle più spinose e più robinie
soprattutto questo odore di foglie nuove
ma come può?
come è possibile
che tutto un mondo si colori di mattino
se vi tengo per mano

PASTEL

to the little ones
Francesca and Caterina

but how can a rabbit
make the meadow greener
a railway line
a red brick station
hide themselves among hills of robinia
to make them more thorny and the more robinia
above all this smell of new leaves
but how can it?
how is it possible
that a whole world grow colored with morning
if I hold you two by the hand

PERCHÉ NON IO

perché non io lungo lo stradale
almeno fino al passaggio a livello
tra i lillà delle ville
della valle del Tanaro
le mie figlie per mano
le scarpe bianche di cuoio
la cintura al buco più largo
perché non io
dopopranzo la sera

WHY NOT ME

why not me along the main road
at least as far as the level crossing
among the lilacs of the villas
in the Tanaro valley
holding my daughters by the hand
with white leather shoes
belt at its broadest hole
why not me
after dinner one evening

FESTA DELLE NAZIONI

Mi ridesta un va e vieni
di bottiglie rovesciate
avanzano le pareti di mogano
nel buio oscilla la notte
le meningi si dolgono agli oblò
come cani alla luna
era cominciato con l'austria
ascesa sul palco, villereccia
aveva danzato con mani sui fianchi, poi
la sorella latina, si attendeva
più brio o ce n'era fin troppo
con gli scozzesi
almeno si pensava alla morte
per quelle tristi nenie
ma l'italia
no, l'italia è un signore in carrozza
col bavero alzato, le lunghe fedine
che tra Colorno e Rubiera
si arresta davanti a una frasca
paga da bere a tutti
se ne va con una lunga frustata al tiro a due
guarda avanti e lontano
prende distanza dalle cose, indietro, molto indietro
fin da quando studiava in seminario
ha sempre qualcosa che non può dire
ma non è facile rappresentare tutto questo
in mezzo all'oceano.

FESTIVAL OF NATIONS

I awake to a coming and going
of overturned bottles
mahogany walls approach
in the dark night wavers
temples howl at the portholes
like dogs at the moon
it began with austria
taking the stage, folk dances
performed with hands on hips, and then
the latin sister, we expected more
brio or there was even too much
with the scots
there were at least thoughts of death
thanks to their mournful drone
but italy
no, italy's a squire in a coach
with collar up, long sideburns
who halts before an inn sign
between Colorno and Rubiera
stands everyone a round of drinks
leaves with a long whip-lash at his two-in-hand
looks forward and far off
keeps things at a distance, behind, far behind,
since his studies in the seminary
always there's something that he cannot say
but it's not so easy to put all this on
in the middle of the ocean.

LE GIOVANI COPPIE

Le giovani coppie del dopoguerra
pranzavano in spazi triangolari
in appartamenti vicini alla fiera
i vetri avevano cerchi alle tendine
i mobili erano lineari, con pochi libri
l'invitato che aveva portato del chianti
bevevamo in bicchieri di vetro verde
era il primo siciliano della mia vita
noi eravamo il suo modello di sviluppo.

THE YOUNG COUPLES ✓

The young couples of the postwar years
would lunch in triangular spaces
of apartments near the fair
the windows had rings on their curtains
the furniture was linear, with hardly any books
the guest who brought Chianti
we drank from green glass tumblers
was the first Sicilian I'd ever met
us, we were his model of development.

NUOVI METODI DEL DOTTOR K

Lei nutre timori irrazionali.
Non deve. Esamini. Rifletta.
Scomponga componga ricomponga
opponga all'evento fredde analisi.

Non so perché, ieri al parco Volta
l'otto volante le giostre i tirasegni
poi il bisogno di urlare di fuggire
di salire su un grande ippocastano.

Se è tutto qui. Prenda un foglio, sottragga
PAURA a LUNAPARK, cosa le resta?
KLN, lo vede, il mondo è suo!
Ci studi sopra, decripti, si diverta.

Non capisco, è un servizio segreto?
un'aerolinea? mi scusi, non capisco.
Proprio così. Quel che conta è lo sforzo.
Lei è guarito. Può andare. Firmi qui.

NEW METHODS OF DOCTOR K

You are nourishing irrational fears.
You mustn't. Consider. Reflect.
Decompose compose recompose
oppose to the event cold analyses.

I don't know why, at Volta Park yesterday
the flying eight the rides the shooting galleries
then the need to cry to run away
to climb up a great horse chestnut tree.

Well if that's all. Take a sheet, subtract
PAURA from LUNAPARK, what've you got left?
KLN, you see, the world's your oyster!
Spend time on it, decode, have fun.

I don't understand, it's a secret service?
An airline? Sorry, but I don't understand.
Just so. What counts is the trying.
You're healed. You can go. Sign here.

MAILAND

bastava
per farci ridere
la fabbrica italiana di ghiaccio artificiale
ma accadeva in certe domeniche di mezza stagione
di grandi nuvole che erano più vaste del cielo
quando al varietà chi sceglievo, si fa per dire
era sempre la ballerina di terza fila
nascosta tra le pieghe dei velari
nell'alterno su e giù della parata
immaginavo di accompagnarla in periferia
tra case nuove dove nelle sere di luna
è più lucente il granito dei marciapiedi
e si fa acuto il taglio degli isolati
la salutavo, della sua pelliccia a buon mercato
mi restava un odore di pelle appena conciata

verità era che mi portavo addosso rientrando
un greve odore di krapfen e di kipfeln
di strapuntini rossi e di tram gialloneri
salivo scale senza ascensore
di piccola gente, di piccola europa

MAILAND V

it was enough
to make us laugh
the Italian artificial ice factory
but it befell on certain middle-season Sundays
with great clouds vaster than the sky
when at the variety the one I selected, let's say,
was always the dancing-girl in the third row
concealed between folds of the curtains
in the alternating ups and downs of the parade
I'd imagine taking her home in the outskirts
between new houses where on moonlit evenings
the pavements' granite is more shiny
and it makes the cut of the flats more acute
I'd tell her goodbye, from her bargain fur coat
an odor of just treated pelt remained

truth was going home myself I'd be wearing
a heavy odor of *krapfen* and *kipfeln*
red cushions and yellow-black trams
I'd be climbing stairs without elevator
of ordinary people, of ordinary europe

IDEA FISSA

antiquam exquirite matrem

Ricordo una montagna inglese
salita fra erbe stillanti
di pioggia marina, e tante mani
e volti lisci e aperti
che vedevo salire sotto me
e pur non ricordando se a quel culmine
sovrastasse un cumulo di sassi
o un rudere di antichissima età
nel ricordo, ma solo nel ricordo,
mi pare di scorgere in un sasso
l'espressione di un volto dolce e muto

chi mi trova quel sasso?

IDÉE FIXE

antiquam exquirite matrem

I remember an English mountain
climbed through grass that dripped
with seaboard rain, and many
smooth and open hands and faces
I saw ascending down below me
and yet not remembering if at the summit
there rose up a stone cumulus
or ruin from most ancient times
in my memory, but in my memory alone,
I seem to make out in a stone
the expression of a sweet, mute face

who finds me that stone?

GLI ADDII

a Francesca

potrebbe essere l'ultima volta che li vedo
mi dici dei tuoi compagni di classe
che ti hanno fatto far tardi
oggi che è finita la scuola
dovrei sgridarti e sto invece a ammirare
i tuoi quaderni bene ordinati
(con qualche sbavatura d'inchiostro
di dita sudate di giochi di giugno)
in autumno andrai alle superiori
e questa tua bella scrittura un po' tonda
potrebbe essere l'ultima volta che la vedo.

THE GOODBYES *V*

to Francesca

it could be the last time I see them
you tell me of your classmates
as they've made you late
today now school is over
I should scold you and instead
I'm admiring your tidy notebooks
(with one or two ink smudges
of fingers sweaty from June games)
you'll go up to high school in autumn
and this pretty rounded hand of yours
it could be the last time I see it.

SETTE E MEZZO

Probabile che tra le sette e le otto
di sera di luglio o d'agosto
ragazzi tra i sette e otto anni
possano capire qualcosa
di questo mondo o dell'altro
giocando in giardini dove crescano
alberi a foglie grigie e bacche rosse . . .
Se mi è capitato? tanto
non avrei saputo che potevo capire
ed ora? ho capito che non posso sapere.

SEVEN AND A HALF

Probably between seven and eight
of an evening in July or August
kids between seven and eight
can understand something
of this world or the other
playing in gardens where trees
with gray leaves and red berries grow . . .
If it happened to me? in any case
I wouldn't have known I could understand
and now? I've understood that I can't know.

from *L'ippopotamo*

The Hippopotamus (1989)

NEL BOSCO

e tu pensavi che come a un saggio orientale
ti bastasse stare addossato a gambe incrociate
alle radici sporgenti di un faggio
per allontanare il pensiero di lei
e diventare l'azzurro tra i rami
o magari formica corteccia filo d'erba

sono passati tre lenti fiocchi di nuvole
e sei ancora tu

ami, ma ami senza:
migliore esperienza?

IN THE WOOD ✓

and you thought that like an Eastern sage
it would be enough to stay leaning cross-legged
at the protruding roots of a beech tree
to distance the thought of her
and become the blue between branches
or perhaps even ant bark blade of grass

three slow flocky clouds have passed
and you are still you

you love, but love without her:
experience, is there any better?

GRAFOLOGIA DI UN ADDIO

Questo azzurro di luglio senza te
è attraversato da troppi neri rondoni
che hanno un colore di antenne
e il taglio, il guizzo della tua scrittura.
Si va dal «caro» alla firma
dal cielo alla terra
dalla prima all'ultima riga
dai tetti alle nuvole.

GRAPHOLOGY OF A GOODBYE ⌄

This blue of a July without you
is crossed by too many black swifts
with the color of antennae
and the cut, the dash of your writing.
They go from the "dear" to the signature
from the sky to the earth
from the first to last line
from the roofs to the clouds.

ISTRIA

Pietra su pietra
poveri muri a secco senza calce
pazienza di secoli
frutti color delle foglie
doline color dell'amore
con quel po' d'acqua che basta
perché attorno al tuffarsi delle mantidi
si allarghino perfettissimi cerchi;
nelle ore calde della giornata
la gente sta seduta
le mani in mano sulla porta di casa,
un gatto gioca col topo
nella polvere della strada di Albona,
una donna cala il secchio nel pozzo
lo ritira fin quasi a metà
lo riaffonda di nuovo . . .
Non pensavo che si potesse fare una lettura
dei segni di questa terra assonnata.

ISTRIA ✓

Stone upon stone
poor dry-stone walls without lime
patience of centuries
fruit the color of leaves
dolines the color of love
with that little water which suffices
because around where the mantises dive
the most perfect circles extend;
in the hot hours of day
the people stay seated
doing nothing at house doors,
cat plays with mouse
in the dust of the Albona road,
a woman drops her bucket in the well
she pulls it up near halfway
she lets it sink once more . . .
I didn't think you could make a reading
from the signs of this drowsy land.

IL PUBBLICO E IL PRIVATO

È entrato aprile in casa con il merlo
che fischia sopra i fili del bucato
è entrato in città il vento ed è passato
sui prati più ingialliti, sotto i ponti
di ferro, come un volo per scommessa
di un biplano dei primi aviatori.
Sulle spallette della sopraelevata
dove uomini in blu hanno fissato
dei lunghi cassoni di cemento
per piantare del verde e qualche fiore
e far più umana la grande città
(ma se neppure un'erba selvatica
ha voglia di attecchire e di fiorire
nei vasi del sindaco sociale!)
il vento ha spazzato tutto quanto
sollevato la polvere e la terra
e ora alza bandiere sui pennoni
laggiù alla fiera internazionale.
Più tardi quando chiudono i mercati
e vanno donne con fresche verdure
(sgusceranno piselli ai ballatoi
tra piante color delle viole
fiorite in pentole smaltate di blu)
mi sembra ruoti il disco solare
tra i tetti di un'altra città.

(anni 1960–70)

THE PUBLIC AND THE PRIVATE

April came inside with the blackbird
whistling above washing lines
wind came into the city and went
over yellower fields, below bridges
of iron, like the gambling flight
of a first aviator's biplane.
On parapets of the overpass
where men in blue have fixed
some long cement boxes to plant
greenery and a few flowers
and make the big city more human
(but if not even a wild tuft of grass
cares to take root and to flower
in vases of the socialist mayor!)
the wind's made a clean sweep
uplifting the dust and the earth
and now raises banners high on the poles
down at the international fair.
Much later when the markets close
and women go home with fresh greens
(they'll shell peas on balconies
between plants the color of violets
flowering in pans enameled with blue)
it seems to me the sun's disc wheels
between a quite other city's roofs.

(1960s–70s)

IL ROCCOLO

Su uno sperone di monte cresceva
un'erba né gialla né nera
un casotto neppure si vedeva
verde tra faggi e betulle
né lontani né troppo vicini
finché da una feritoia partì un colpo
e apparve un lungo essere nero
a raccogliere un uccellino caduto da un ramo secco
un essere come quei magri che nei western portano un cilindro
e fabbricano casse da morto sulla main street:
ma questo era bergamasco e coadiutore
e se vado ancora per preti
è più che mai per una questione di equilibri
direi qui per un gusto di colori
di verde di polenta e di nero.
Che se poi volete saperne di più
andate a trovare il Pfarrer Johann Hämmerle
che in una certa valle delle Alpi
coltiva fiori di altissimo stelo
di petali azzurri e stellati:
devo dire che il miele delle sue api ha un sapore sui generis.
Pare che questi fiori
(ma chi si fida dei preti)
siano stati trapiantati
da non so qual pianoro dell'Asia Centrale.

THE BIRD TRAP

On a spur of mountain grew
a grass neither black nor yellow
a hide you couldn't even see
green between beech and birch trees
not distant nor too near
until from the loophole a shot came
and there appeared a tall black being
to gather a little bird dropped from a dry bough
a being like those thin types wearing top hats in westerns
who knock together coffins on main street:
but this was a curate and from Bergamo
and if I go looking for priests still
it's more than ever a question of balances
here I'd say a taste for colors
for green for bright yellow and for black.
And if you want to know more of it
go find the Reverend Johann Hämmerle
who grows in a certain Alpine valley
flowers with such lofty stems
with blue and starry petals:
I must say his bees' honey has a taste all its own.
It seems these flowers
(but who trusts priests)
they were transplanted
from I don't know what Central Asian plateau.

RICHIUDENDO UN BAULE

Quel berrettuccio di lana vergine
bianco grigio e marrone
comprato in un folto di abeti
da un'indiana della riserva Sioux
(starà bene alla seconda bambina
che ha un taglio d'occhi un po' samoiedi)
anni dopo lo ritrovo in fondo a un baule
di un'umida casa in campagna.
Neppure messo una volta
sembra ora un passato di castagne
quasi un mont-blanc, ma seduto.
E dire che l'indiana aveva sorriso
accarezzato il cavallo
e che il sole tra gli alberi . . .
Ma addio Montagne Rocciose
hand knitted original article!

(1975)

CLOSING A TRUNK ONCE MORE ✓

That nice little beret of virgin wool
white gray and brown
bought in a stand of firs
from an Indian girl on the Sioux reservation
(it'll look good on the second child
who's got eyes slightly Samoyede-shaped)
I found it years later at the bottom of a trunk
in a damp house in the country.
Not even worn once
now it seems a chestnut purée
almost a mont-blanc, but flopped down.
And to say that the Indian girl had smiled
stroked the horse
and that the sun among the trees . . .
But goodbye Rocky Mountain
"hand knitted original article!"

(1975)

SUITE AMERICANA

C'è da dire
che eravamo entusiasti del nostro nuovo cappello di pelo
sulla diagonale spazzata dal vento
né del tutto infelici
tra tavoli bisunti di salsicce
inondati di birra, sopra il ferry,
che si andasse all'ovest o verso est.
La bambina biondo oro
in corsa sull'ammezzato
rischiosamente vicino a balconate di ferro battuto
che davano su una hall piena di luci
e i palmizi di un grande magazzino
non ne sa niente, non ricorderà
la pista nel bosco, cancellata
dalle betulle cadute di traverso,
e neppure tutte le rughe del vecchio hardware di N. B.
che si spianavano al solo vederla
mentre mi vendeva chiodi di diversa misura.
Un mattino arriva un merlo di tre colori
un merlo d'oltremare
che m'invita a tornare.

(1978)

SUITE AMERICANA ✓

It's worth saying
we weren't unenthusiastic about our new fur hat
on the diagonal swept by wind
nor entirely unhappy
among tables greased with sausages
awash with beer, on the ferry,
whether we were going west or towards east.
The golden blonde baby girl
running on the mezzanine
riskily near the wrought-iron rail
giving onto a hall of lights
and the palm fronds of a department store
knows nothing about it, won't recall
the track in the wood, rubbed out
by the birch trees fallen across it,
and equally all the wrinkles on the old "hardware of N. B." man
smoothed away at the very sight of her
while he sold me nails of various sizes.
One morning a three-colored blackbird arrives
a blackbird from over the seas
inviting me to go back home.

(1978)

QUARTIERE SOLARI

Milano ha tramonti rosso oro.
Un punto di vista come un altro
erano gli orti di periferia
dopo i casoni della «Umanitaria».
Tra siepi di sambuco e alcuni uscioli
fatti di latta e di imposte sconnesse,
l'odore di una fabbrica di caffè
si univa al lontano sentore delle fonderie.
Per quella ruggine che regnava invisibile
per quel sole che scendeva più vasto
in Piemonte in Francia chissà dove
mi pareva di essere in Europa;
mia madre sapeva benissimo
che non le sarei stato a lungo vicino
eppure sorrideva
su uno sfondo di dalie e viole ciocche.

(1978)

QUARTIERE SOLARI ✓

Milan has sunsets of a golden red.
A point of view like any other
the allotments on the outskirts were
after the *Umanitaria*'s flat blocks.
Among elder hedges and a few wicket gates
made of tin and ill-fitting shutters,
the smell of a coffee factory
mingled with the distant odor of the foundries.
For that rust which reigned invisible
for that sun which went down vaster
in Piedmont in France who knows where
it seemed to me I was in Europe;
my mother knew only too well
that I wouldn't be a long time near her
she was smiling nonetheless
on a background of dahlias and clustered violets.

(1978)

FINE DELLE VACANZE

Ero uno che sollevava la pietra
affondata nell'erba tra la malva
scoprendo un mondo di radicole bianche
di città color verde pisello;
ma partite le ultime ragazze
che ancora ieri erano ferme in bicicletta
nascoste da grandi foglie di settembre
alle sbarre del passaggio a livello
mi sento io stesso quella pietra.
Anche le nuvole sono basse sui campi di tennis
e il nome dell'hotel scritto sul muro
a nere, grandi lettere è tutto intriso di pioggia.

END OF THE HOLIDAYS

I was one who would lift up a stone
sunk in grass between the mallow
to discover a world with little white roots
of a pea-green colored city;
but the last of the young girls gone
who even yesterday were still on bicycles
hidden by the large September leaves
at the level-crossing's barrier
me I feel myself to be that stone.
Even the clouds are low over the tennis courts
and the hotel name written on the wall
in large black letters is entirely drenched with rain.

ABITO A TRENTA METRI DAL SUOLO

Abito a trenta metri dal suolo
in un casone di periferia
con un terrazzo e doppi ascensori.
Questo era cielo, mi dico
attraversato secoli fa
forse da una fila di aironi
con sotto tutta la falconeria
dei Torriani, magari degli Erba
e bei cavalli in riva agli acquitrini.
Questo mio alloggio e altri alloggi
libri stoviglie inquilini
questo era azzurro, era spazio
luogo di nuvole e uccelli.
L'aria è la stessa: è la stessa?
sopravvivere: vivere sopra?
Non so come mi sento agganciato
la sera ha tempo di farsi più blu
da un pallido re pescatore
o, di passaggio qui in alto,
dal vero barone di Münchhausen.

I LIVE THIRTY METERS FROM THE GROUND ✔

I live thirty meters from the ground
in a building in the suburbs
with a terrace and two lifts.
This was sky, I tell myself
crossed over centuries back
perhaps by a flight of herons
with below it all the falconry
of the Torrianis, the Erbas even
and fine horses on the margins of ponds.
This lodging of mine and other lodgings
books tenants kitchenware
this was azure, it was space
place of clouds and birds.
The air's the same: it's the same?
to survive: to live above?
I don't know how I feel myself hooked
evening has time to become more blue
from a pale fisher king
or, passing up above here,
from the real Baron Münchhausen.

SE NON FOSSE

Se non fosse per queste piccole cifre
per queste ultime e umili cifre
un tempo si sarebbe detto centesimi
per le quali il totale delle entrate
non fa rima con quello delle uscite
e non quadra il bilancio di fine d'anno
(la nebbia sta invadendo le terrazze
ma il fumo sale dritto sopra i tetti?
gli immigrati lanciano petardi
que le blanc ne se casse, mi raccomando)
se non fosse per queste minime cifre
ma discordi, e che fanno la spia
non si starebbe a risalire i conteggi
per trovare il nodo, il principium erroris
la smagliatura, il 5 per un 6
(ma la svista era un 8 per un 3)
non si avrebbe l'eureka, né la folle discesa
per le scritture, né l'arrivo in volata
sino all'abbraccio del dare e dell'avere:
ora saltino i tappi di spumante
e sia zero anche questo
mio ennesimo dì di San Silvestro.

(1978)

IF IT WEREN'T

If it weren't for these small numbers
for these last and humble numbers
one time we'd have called them cents
thanks to which the total income
doesn't rhyme with that outgoing
and the balance won't square at year's end
(fog is invading the balconies
but smoke rises straight up over roofs?
the immigrants hurl firecrackers
que le blanc ne se casse, don't forget)
if it weren't for these tiny but discordant
numbers, ones that give the game away
we wouldn't be redoing the accounts
to find the knot, principium erroris
the stocking ladder, the 5 for a 6
(but the oversight was an 8 for a 3)
nor would we have the eureka, nor mad descent
through the entries, nor final sprint
right to the embrace of the give and take:
now have the corks fly from the bubbly
and make it zero even this
umpteenth New Year's Eve of mine.

(1978)

SE È TUTTO QUI ...

Turbano la mia limpida fede
cattolica apostolica e che più
non tanto il corso dei tempi
il tradimento dei nuovi chierici, i magnifici scandali
mi restano in mano altri pezzi del puzzle
ad esempio il povero vitello grasso
che sarà l'unico ad andare di mezzo
quando il figliolo prodigo si deciderà a ritornare.
Chiaro che non ho capito niente
che dovrò ancora pensarci un po' su.

IF THIS IS ALL . . .

They disturb my limpid faith
catholic apostolic and whatever else
not so much the course of the times
the new clerks' treason, magnificent scandals
other bits of the puzzle remain in my hand
for example the poor fatted calf
that will be the one to suffer
when the prodigal decides to return.
I have obviously understood nothing
will have to think on it again some more.

L'IO E IL NON IO

diagonalmente abeti verso il cielo
mentre sopra l'abisso d'aria viola
il codafolta va di ramo in ramo
ed io con lui verso rupi rosate
mentalmente
saltellando tra me di palo in frasca

THE I AND NOT-I ✓

diagonally fir trees towards the sky
while over the abyss of violet air
the bushy-tail goes from bough to bough
and I'm with him towards pink rocks
mentally
skipping to myself beside one point and another

QUANDO PENSO A MIA MADRE

Nulla ho scritto di te quando sei andata
e poco ho scritto dopo, il lungo dopo.
Ritorni solo nei sogni di ogni notte
o, il giorno, a caso, nell'aria di via B
dopo che è nevicato e si respira;
o in una luce pomeridiana di persiane socchiuse
e vi è un fruscìo di giornale di grande formato;
o in qualche nome di luogo che mi si ferma in gola.
Tutto qui? non accetto la morte, mi si dice.
È vero, non riapro i tuoi cassetti, non rileggo
le tue lettere. Che io sia
nient'altro che una pietra
un Giovannino heartless?
Quanto tempo mi resterà ancora per imparare
a sorridere e amare come te?

(1978–83)

WHEN I THINK OF MY MOTHER ✓

I wrote nothing of you after you'd gone
and I've written little since, the long time since.
You only return in dreams of every night
or, daytime, by chance, in the air of via B
after it's snowed and one can breathe;
or in an afternoon light of half-closed blinds
and there's a rustle of large newspapers;
or in some place-name that sticks in the throat.
That's all? I don't accept death, they tell me.
It's true, I don't reopen your drawers, don't reread
your letters. As if
I were no more than a stone,
a little Johnny heartless?
How much time remains to me still
for learning how to smile and love like you?

(1978–83)

UNA VISITA A CALEPPIO

Tra donne nate per tirare carri
mi sento nascosto come un fungo
in acque basse in cerca di conchiglie
la gamba più all'asciutto è la più scarna
soltanto nell'immagine del padre
giovinetto, vestito da collegio,
o attento a ascoltare «Parla Londra!»
da una radio che sembra un tabernacolo
riesco e mi piace riconoscermi.
Tempo e luogo? ma forse
un novembre di vino e di castagne;
lontano, nel silenzio della bassa,
un landò nero passa oltre le rogge,
lievi calessi accarezzano le strade
già indurite dal freddo. Gli antenati?
In cielo e in terra molte cose, Horatio . . .
dunque nel novero degli eventi improbabili
niente è proprio impossibile, perfino
ritrovarti, confonderci tutti
in questo mare di nebbia sulle risaie.

A VISIT TO CALEPPIO ✓

Among women born to pull carts
I feel I'm hidden like a mushroom
in shallow water in search of shells
the drier leg is the skinnier one
only in the picture of the young
father, rigged out for college,
or intent on hearing "London Calling!"
from a radio that seems a tabernacle
I'm able and happy to recognize myself.
Time and place? well maybe
a November of wine and chestnuts;
far distant, in the silence of the lowlands,
a black landau goes by beyond ditches,
light calashes caress the roads
already hardened by cold. The forebears?
There are more things in heaven and earth, Horatio . . .
therefore in the class of improbable events
nothing's truly impossible, not even
to find yourself again, to confuse everyone
in this sea of fog upon the rice fields.

IMPLOSION

Dicembre mi ha dischiuso una finestra
nel giro che fa il Sole attorno all'Anno:
è uno spaccato freddo, ma sul fondo
vi è una tavola bianca apparecchiata.

Pranzi di Natale, ma io dov'ero?
a destra del nonno socialista?
abbiamo tutti un nonno socialista
il mio diceva «l'Odio è stolto» e aggiungeva
a noi rivolto «Ombre dal volo breve!»
(sulle guance
quando uscivamo nel cielo blu notte
rabbrividiva l'ultima arancia).

Il cerchio è aperto, la tavola ha una falla
lo spiraglio è più bianco meno freddo
chi cerco resta sempre alle mie spalle.

IMPLOSION

December's prized open a window for me
in the course the Sun makes round the Year:
it's a cold sliver, but in the background
there's a white table been laid.

Christmas dinners, but me where was I?
to the right of my socialist granddad?
we all have a socialist granddad
mine was saying "Hate's foolish" and added
"Fleeting shadows!" meaning us
(on our cheeks
when we went out into blue night sky
the final orange shivered).

The circle's open, the table has a leak
the gleam is whiter, less cold
she's always at my back, the one I seek.

PONTE E CITTÀ

riattraversarlo vorrebbe anche se oscilla
periglioso, sospeso sull'abisso
non importa se manca qualche asse
tra le corde stanche e sfilacciate
se il vento che soffia nella gola
fa trepido e incerto il suo passaggio
vorrebbe metter piede all'altra sponda
sponda come? di un'erba calpestata
un po' verde, un po'gialla, di città
di sobborgo, non landa né steppa
quali umani? se stesso nei passanti
per vie di pioggia, di negozi chiusi
tra facciate notturne di finestre
illuminate di ussari, di musiche
né mai chiedersi a un angolo di strada
ed io, io, ospite di quale sera?

BRIDGE AND CITY ✓

he'd wanted to cross it again even though
it dangerously sways, hung above the abyss
no matter if some slats are missing
between the worn out and frayed ropes
if the wind that blows in the gorge makes
his crossing fearful and uncertain
he'd wanted to set foot on the far bank
which bank? one of trampled grass
a bit green, a bit yellow, a city's
a suburb's, neither moor nor steppe
which humans? himself among the passersby
through streets of rain, of closed shops
between night façades with windows
illuminated by hussars, by music
nor ever ask himself at a corner of the street
and me, me, guest of which evening?

FILO DI FERRO

mi hanno detto che sono un filo di ferro
perché magro svelto resistente
invece no e lo sapevamo da ragazzi
che per spezzare un filo di ferro
se non hai pinze basta piegarlo di qua
e poi di là tre quattro sei volte
così mi chiedo davanti a una parete
se non sia oggi la mia settima volta
una parete dove il suo profilo
non si modella più, non si delineano
alla luce serale della lampada
la sua fronte il suo mento le sue labbra
una parete bianca

IRON WIRE ✓

they told me I'm an iron wire
because thin sharp resistant
but not really and we learned as boys
that to break an iron wire
if you haven't any pincers only bend it
this way and that three four six times
just so, I wonder in front of a wall
if it isn't my seventh time today
a wall where her profile's
modeled no longer, no longer outlined
by the evening lamplight
are her chin her lips her forehead
a wall entirely white

SEGUIVO IL TUO VIAGGIO

seguivo il tuo viaggio
provavo le tue impressioni
pensavo i tuoi pensieri
meglio del simulatore di un centro spaziale
che riproduce a terra le vicende
di un'astronave in volo tra le stelle
finché scese le ombre sopra i tetti
te addormentata, perso ogni contatto
caddi di quota, riabitai un mio baratro
tra voci inascoltate e la spezzata
illusione di un filo che legasse
non solo a te ma a ogni cosa sperata
ai grandi assenti, a eterni *invisibilia*

I WAS FOLLOWING YOUR JOURNEY

I was following your journey
having your impressions
I was thinking your thoughts
better than a space center simulator
producing on earth the adventures
of a spaceship flying amid stars
till shadows fallen on the roofs
you gone to sleep, all contact lost
I dropped down, was back in my abyss
among voices unheeded and the broken
illusion of a thread that would tether me
not just to you but to every hoped-for thing
to the great absent ones, the everlasting *invisibles*

IL TRANVIERE METAFISICO

Ritorna a volte il sogno in cui mi avviene
di manovrare un tram senza rotaie
tra campi di patate e fichi verdi
nel coltivato le ruote non sprofondano
schivo spaventapasseri e capanni
vado incontro a settembre, verso ottobre
i passeggeri sono i miei defunti.
Al risveglio rispunta il dubbio antico
se questa vita non sia evento del caso
e il nostro solo un povero monologo
di domande e risposte fatte in casa.
Credo, non credo, quando credo vorrei
portarmi all'al di là un po' di qua
anche la cicatrice che mi segna
una gamba e mi fa compagnia.
Già, ma allora? sembra dica *in excelsis*
un'altra voce.
Altra?

THE METAPHYSICAL TRAMDRIVER

Sometimes the dream returns where it happens
I'm maneuvering a tram without rails
through fields of potatoes and green figs
the wheels don't sink in the crops
I avoid bird-scarers and huts
go to meet September, towards October
the passengers are my own dead.
At waking there comes back the ancient doubt
if this life weren't a chance event
and our own just a poor monologue
of homemade questions and answers.
I believe, don't believe, when believing I'd like
to take to the beyond with me a bit of the here
even the scar that marks my leg
and keeps me company.
Sure, and so? another voice *in excelsis*
appears to say.
Another?

L'IPPOPOTAMO

forse la galleria che si apre
l'ippopotamo nel folto della giungla
per arrivare al fiume, ai curvi pascoli
di foglie nate a forma di cuore

forse il varco tra alberi e liane
gli ostacoli divelti, le improvvise
irruzioni d'azzurro nelle tenebre
su un umido scempio di orchidee

forse questo e qualsiasi tracciato
come a Parigi la Neuilly-Vincennes
o l'umile «infiorata» di Genzano

o un canale di Marte, altro non sono
che eventi privi d'ombra e di riflesso
soltanto un segno che segna se stesso

THE HIPPOPOTAMUS ✓

perhaps the tunnel that the hippopotamus
opens in the thick of the jungle
to arrive at the river, at the sloped pastures
of leaves created heart-shaped

perhaps the passage between trees and lianas
the obstacles uprooted, unforeseen
outbreaks of azure in the shades
on a damp trampling of orchids

perhaps this and any such trackway
as in Paris the Neuilly-Vincennes
or Genzano's humble "flower show"

or a canal on Mars, are none other
than events without shadow or reflection
just a sign signaling itself alone

LA VIDA ES ...

(rileggendo il Parini)

La corsa allegra del trasporto pubblico
il pie' non dubitante a curve e arresti
la stessa calca, se una donna sorride,
fasciati di cretonne gli arditi fianchi,
tanto basta all'anziano passeggero
per sentirsi rivivere un istante
(ma anche un coro di Verdi o certa luce
tra le foglie ai giardini della Guastalla).

Né se un giovine onesto dice «prego
s'accomodi», è gran male perché il gioco
delle parti è previsto e manifesto
anzi l'anziano prende posto fiero
di questa ritrovata dignità
nel balletto degli usi e dei costumi.

Ma se a dire «s'accomodi» è un teppista
o peggio uno di quelli che vorrebbero
cambiare il mondo con barba e bisaccia,
l'invito suona come una sentenza
di morte senza appello. Le mie rughe,
si dice il passeggero, il crin canuto,
le mie spalle cadenti hanno commosso
perfino questo pseudo proletario.

E perché tutti torni come prima
il sole il mondo l'oggi e l'illusione
occorre che frenando il mezzo pubblico
il giaccone verdastro dell'irsuto
s'accoppii coi fiori del cretonne
nella valle di Giosafat di un autobus
in corsa, giallo, sotto gli ippocastani.

LA VIDA ES . . .

(rereading Parini)

The municipal bus's cheerful route
the foot unfaltering at corners and stops
the usual crowd, if a woman should smile,
her daring flanks bandaged with cretonne,
so much is enough for the old passenger
to feel himself come back to life for a moment
(but a chorus from Verdi or certain light too
through leaves in the Guastalla gardens).

Or should a well-meaning young man say "Please
do sit down," no it's not a great evil because
the roles are foreseen and quite clear
the old one indeed takes the seat with pride
with that rediscovered dignity
in the ballet of customs and habits.

But if it's some yahoo that says "Do sit down"
or, worse, one of those who would wish
to change the world with knapsack and beard,
the gesture just sounds like a sentence
of death without leave to appeal. My wrinkles,
the passenger says to himself, my white mane,
my burdened-down shoulders have moved
even this pseudo-proletarian.

And for all to return as before
the sun the world the day and illusion
what's needed is that as the vehicle brakes
the big greenish jacket of the bearded man
should be matched with the flowers of cretonne
in this bus's valley of Jehosaphat
on its journey, yellow, beneath the chestnut trees.

IRREVERSIBILITÀ

Fu più di un grido: Coglili col gambo lungo!
ranuncoli doppi, ranuncoli gialli
dove il fiume rinasce
sull'argine si cammina tra due acque.
Più di un grido e altre albe
quando il diamante assai raro
sanguina nei vapori di aprile
sul sonno di una nuova città.
Aspettami!
Ti sei allontanato tra i noccioli.

(1963)

IRREVERSIBILITY

It was more than a cry: Pick ones with long stems!
double buttercups, yellow buttercups
where the river's reborn
on the bank you walk between two waters.
More than a cry and other dawns
when the so rare diamond
bleeds in the vapors of April
upon a new city's sleep.
Wait for me!
You've taken yourself off through the nut trees.

(1963)

QUALE MILANO?

La cartolina tra i raggi della ruota
imitava un suono di motore
quando in via XX Settembre
si scendeva dal Parco in bicicletta:
perché a Milano, per biliardo che sia
vi sono strade in salita e in discesa
più frequenti nei sogni e nei ricordi
specie se legate a un primo incontro
a un saluto guantato di viola.

WHICH MILAN? ✓

The postcard in the spokes of the wheel
would imitate the sound of an engine
when in via XX Settembre
we'd go down from the Park by bike:
because in Milan, a billiard table as might be
there are streets that climb and descend
more often in dreams and in memories
especially if linked with a first meeting
with a violet-gloved greeting.

AUTORITRATTO

Uomo vecchio in città
disperso su tronchi secondari di ferrovia
o con un piatto di lesso
davanti a tetti umidi di pioggia.

Tutto qui il tuo qui e ora?
Interroghi l'alfabeto delle cose
ma al tuo non capire niente di ogni sera
sai la risposta di un mazzo di rose?

Rimani quello che andava per ciliege
e a mani vuote
strappava al tronco nastri di corteccia.

Resti un ladro di polli
con gli occhi oggi ancora sprovveduti
di quando in ritardo andavi a scuola.

SELF-PORTRAIT ✓

Old man in town
missing on railway branch lines
or with a plate of boiled meats
before roofs wet with rain.

Nothing else your here and now?
You're questioning the alphabet of things
but uncomprehending each evening
you know a bunch of roses' reply?

You're no less the one who went after cherries
and empty-handed
would rip bark ribbons off the trunks.

You remain a chicken thief
with eyes today unwary still
as when you'd be off to school late.

MOTUS IN FINE VELOCIOR

anche tu aspetti il fischio dell'arbitro
come quei calciatori
che ottenuto un vantaggio di reti
rallentano il gioco in attesa
che scada il tempo della partita
non ti ha insegnato niente la tua squadra
quella che stava vincendo
scendeva la nebbia sullo stadio
e fu veloce, anzi più veloce alla fine
era l'Inter
una volta tanto

MOTUS IN FINE VELOCIOR ✓

you too await the referee's whistle
like those soccer players
who've got a goal advantage
and so slow the play down
waiting for full time
your team's not taught you anything
the one that was winning
fog descended on the stadium
and they were fast, faster even at the end
it was Inter
at least this once

from *L'ipotesi circense*

The Circus Hypothesis (1995)

UN COSMO QUALUNQUE

Abitano mondi intermedi
spazi di fisica pura
le cose senza prestigio
gli oggetti senza *design*
la cravatta per il mio compleanno
le *Trabant* dei paesi dell'est.
Turbano, ma che mai vorrà dire?
Forse meglio di altri
esprimono una loro tensione
un'aura, si diceva una volta
verso quanto qui ci circonda.

ANY OLD COSMOS ✓

They live in intermediate worlds
spaces of pure physics
these things without prestige
objects with no *design*
the necktie for my birthday
the eastern block's *Trabant*.
They trouble, but whatever does it mean?
Maybe better than others
they express a tension of their own
an aura, as we used to say
towards what's surrounding us here.

AUTUNNALE

Seduto sulla panchina di un parco
di una città popolosa
di operai senza rivoluzione
come quando in Crimea
come quando al tramonto
non mi va più di partire
resto in uno squarcio di giallo
di un viale ghiaioso
ma chi passa si accorge
di questo odore di fuochi in novembre?

AUTUMNAL ✓

Sitting on a park bench
in a populous city
of workers with no revolution
as when in the Crimea
as when at the sun's going down
I don't feel like leaving anymore
I remain in the yellow gash
of a gravely avenue
but the ones going past are aware
of this scent of fires in November?

SENZA BUSSOLA

Secondo Darwin avrei dovuto essere eliminato
secondo Malthus neppure essere nato
secondo Lombroso finirò comunque male
e non sto a dire di Marx, io, *petit bourgeois*
scappare, dunque, scappare
in avanti in dietro di fianco
(così nel quaranta quando tutti) ma
permangono personali perplessità
sono a est della mia ferita
o a sud della mia morte?

WITHOUT A COMPASS ✓

According to Darwin I'd not be of the fittest
according to Malthus not even born
according to Lombroso I'll end bad anyway
and not to mention Marx, me, *petit bourgeois*
running for it, therefore, running for it
forward backward sideways
(as in nineteen-forty when everybody) but
there remain personal perplexities
am I to the east of my wound
or to the south of my death?

GENIUS LOCI

Nel primo centenario di Campana
fui invitato a Marradi per un convegno.
Tra le pareti umide e scrostate
di una stanza d'albergo che sapeva
di muffa e di marroni, ossia castagne
ebbi voglia di un amore di passo
o di morire come un commesso viaggiatore.

GENIUS LOCI √

At Campana's first centenary
I was invited to Marradi for a conference.
Between the damp and peeling walls
of a hotel room with smells
of mold and marrons, that's to say chestnuts
I had been wanting a casual affair
or to die like a traveling salesman.

OFF LIMITS FOR DOCTOR K

Non sanno le donne, no, non sanno
che cosa mi fa pensare a loro
insistentemente (è un esempio)
la ricordavo che bagnava i fiori
con un annaffiatoio da bambini;
a volte basta meno, quasi un niente
una donna di spalle
una strada tra i campi
quanto ad analizzare, il ciel ne scampi.

OFF LIMITS FOR DOCTOR K

The women don't know, no, they don't know
what it is makes me think of them
compulsively (it's an example)
I remember her drenching flowers
with a child's watering can;
less'll do often, practically nothing
a woman seen from behind
a road through meadows
as for analyzing, god forbid.

QUESTI ULTIMI ANNI

Questi ultimi anni avuti in premio
hanno a volte il gusto un poco sfatto
di certe scatolette di tonno
che si mangiano ai bordi di un torrente
sull'erba corta, dopo una camminata:
il vino è fresco
la bottiglia tra sassi e corrente.

THESE LAST YEARS ✓

These last years given as a bonus
at times have the faintly "off" taste
of occasional tins of tuna
eaten by the banks of a torrent
on short grass, after taking a stroll:
the wine's chilled
the bottle in among stones and current.

SOLTANTO SEGNI?

I

Sul crocefisso che mi è apparso in sogno
un corpo d'ebano su una croce d'argento
non c'era INRI ma qualcosa come
SP e forse poi QR
a metà del risveglio vorrei credere
che l'iscrizione fosse invece SPES
Segni? Parole? Oppure res?

II

Prima che mi scendesse sopra gli occhi
un sonno dei più pesanti che ricordi
ho visto, ho creduto di vedere
ma che cosa? non so. Quello che resta
è un tratteggio animato, un poco elettrico
di colori sottili, luminosi
come se si volesse cancellare
(da *cancellum*, barriera, anzi steccato)
quello che ho visto e ho dimenticato.

III

Se quello che esiste è preverbale
luci linee colori senza nome
nient'altro che luce, linee e colori
come spiego Giovanni 1/1
In principio era il Verbo
(o il Cantabrico fiero del suo word-world)?

ONLY SIGNS?

I

On the crucifix appearing in a dream to me
an ebony body on a silver cross
there was no INRI but something
like SP and then perhaps QR
half-awake I'd want to believe
instead that the inscription was SPES
Signs? Words? Or res?

II

Before there descended upon my eyes
one of the heaviest dreams I recall
I saw, I believed I saw
well what? Don't know. What remains
is animated hatching, slightly electric
with delicate colors, luminous
as if someone wanted to cancel
(from *cancellum*, "barrier" or better "fence")
what it was I saw and have forgotten.

III

If what exists is preverbal
lights lines colors without name
nothing else but lights, lines and colors
how do I explain John 1 verse 1
In the beginning was the Word
(or the Cantabridgian proud of his word-world)?

DASEIN

L'essere perentorio (*Dasein?*)
del tappeto o di un listello di parquet
mi fa dopo un po' pensare al nulla
quasi stessi leggendo, anzi, assai meglio,
i detti di un saggio tibetano:
un nulla di pelle, direi un brivido
che fa chiudere gli occhi, per vedere
su creste e cornici di monte
andare come se non andassero i treni,
o me stesso con un cappello di paglia
che pedalo diretto al mercato
in sella a una bicicletta da donna:
una strada un po' bianca un po' piana
esserci, allora?

DASEIN ✓

The peremptory being (*Dasein?*)
of the carpet or a fillet of parquet
after a while makes me think of nothingness
almost as if I were reading, indeed, far better,
the pronouncements of a tibetan sage:
a nothingness of skin, let's say a shiver
that closes the eyes, so as to see
over hill crests or ledges
to go as if the trains weren't running,
or myself with a straw hat on
pedaling straight to market
on the saddle of a lady's bicycle:
a road a bit white a bit flat
being there, so then?

A SCUOLA DI SGUARDO

Le stanghette sono molli e sbilenche
le lenti opache e graffiate
a fatica si legge il giornale
se ne vale la pena.
Certi occhiali, ecco il punto,
non sono fatti per vedere
ma per essere visti
sono quelli caduti in una rissa, o
in un cassetto il pince-nez di mio nonno
(i miei li misi al ginnasio
non leggevo le minuscole greche)
addirittura vi sono occhiali che parlano
quelli a mucchi dei campi di sterminio
quelli della nuotatrice, su uno scoglio.

ÉCOLE DU REGARD ✓

The bars are twisted and weak
the lenses scratched and opaque
reading the paper's a struggle
if it's worth the effort.
Some pairs of glasses, here's the point,
aren't made for seeing
but being seen
there are those fallen off in a brawl, or
my granddad's pince-nez in a drawer
(mine I wore at high school
I wasn't reading the lowercase Greek)
there are even glasses that speak
those in heaps at extermination camps
those of the swimming girl, up on a rock.

L'IPOTESI CIRCENSE

Ma dove siete Rosencrantz e Guildenstern?
dove pause, *entractes*, ore vuote?
particelle del nulla
se foste voi
a possedere la lampada di Aladino
se figuraste
la morte dalle labbra opache
quella sul viottolo d'erba ingiallita
dello sguardo dai vetri: una spallata,
ma la posta non è appena arrivata?

Comparse, interludi insignificanti
forse è grazie a voi
che non cade il Funambolo.

THE CIRCUS HYPOTHESIS 𝘝

But Rosencrantz and Guildenstern, where are you?
where intervals, *entr'actes*, empty hours?
particles of nothingness
if it were you
who possessed Aladdin's lamp
if you gave form
to Death with the opaque lips
that one on the yellowed-grass path
with the glance from windows: a shrug,
but hasn't the mail just come?

Extras, unmeaning interludes
it's thanks to you perhaps
that the Tightrope walker doesn't fall.

SUITE FERROVIARIA

1942

Siepe di robinia
che segui la strada ferrata
ti lascio i miei pensieri
sulle tue foglie verdi, sottili.
Sul treno che mi portava veloce
a quest'ora del tramonto
pensavo al mio destino
povero, meraviglioso
al cammino
che non so se farò.
Ma mi accompagna il tuo verde filare, ora
lo guardo
e la campagna stanca:
così spesso fuggono
sogni e visioni del mio viaggiare.

1943

Leggevo negli occhi dei famuli
il mio destino la mia certa condanna
andavo in montagna
scarponi e paltò
volevo fuggire
l'Italia e Salò.

1944

Sei nel Giura e guardi dal treno
il convento in mezzo agli abeti
chi è in preghiera? la suora toriera
o il ragazzo che va alla frontiera?

RAILWAY SUITE $\sqrt{}$

1942

Robinia hedge
following the tracks
I leave you my thoughts
on your thin, green leaves.
On the train that carried me
fast at this sunset hour
I was thinking of my poor
marvelous destiny
of the walk
that I don't know if I'll make.
But your green line goes with me, now
I look at it
and at the weary countryside:
just so often flee
dreams and visions of my journey.

1943

I was reading in the eyes of farmhands
my destiny my sure condemnation
in the mountains I would go
hiking boots and overcoat
I was wanting to flee
Italy and Salò.

1944

You're in the Jura and look from the train
at the convent among the beech trees
who is at prayer? the turn-box nun
or boy heading for the frontier?

RINCORRENDO VITTORIO S
SULLA STRADA DI ZENNA

I vecchi il fischio del treno
lontano in corsa nella pianura
lo credevano un segno di maltempo
se passava una nuvola sul sole
ecco, dicevano, *s'annuvola il Signore.*
Io questi brividi di abeti
prima che dalla valle venga il vento
io questo tremito di foglie
dico è un messaggio, qualcuno lo coglie.

CHASING VITTORIO S
ON THE ZENNA ROAD

The old believed a distant train
whistle as it ran through the plain
was a sign of worsening weather
if a cloud passed in front of the sun
see, they'd say, *the Lord clouds over.*
Me these shivering beech trees
before the wind comes from the valley
me these trembling leaves
I say it's a message, somebody receives.

ALTROVE PADANO

I

La vecchia locomotiva di Voghera
arrugginisce ancora sui binari . . .
che siano versi di cantautore?
quali altri versi allora
per questo professore di ginnasio
che dà ripetizioni di latino
tra sassifraghe e frasche
in una villetta con giardino, o
per l'ora del tè dei veterani
a turno vicino al freddo dell'inverno
che da queste parti comincia a farsi sentire
già dopo la Madonna di settembre?

II

Viaggiatore che guardi il tuo treno
in corsa tra le risaie
affacciato da un vagone di coda
in curva tra le robinie,
sei in fuga lungo un arco di spazio?

o immobile guardi lontano
più lontano, da una piega del tempo
se il sole che ora declina
(il verde è un trionfo di giallo)
si arresta ai tuoi occhi pavesi?

Viaggiatore di fine giornata
di collo magro, di fronte stempiata!

PO PLAIN ELSEWHERE

I

Voghera's old locomotive
rusts still on its rails . . .
could be a singer-songwriter's lines?
what other lines then
for this grammar-school master
giving catch-up Latin lessons
amid saxifrage and bushes
in a little villa with garden, or
for the veterans' teatime by turns
towards the chill of winter
starting to make itself felt in these parts
beyond the September Madonna already?

II

Traveler watching your train
on its way through rice fields
looking from a rear carriage
as it curves through robinia,
you're in flight along an arc of space?

or motionless watching afar
farther off, from a fold of time
if the sun descending now
(the green's a triumph of yellow)
remains in your eyes from Pavia?

Traveler at the day's decline
with thin neck, receding hairline!

IL CIRCO

Un circo è un circo, anche un piccolo circo.
Il mio paese sembrava più leggero
la sera, quando issata l'alta cupola
le bandiere si alzavano nel cielo,

quando un drin drin di giochi e carabattole
faceva più spediti il cuore e i passi
i colori apparivano più veri
nell'aria nuova, era marzo, era la sera,

soprattutto l'azzurro, la lontana
linea dei monti, il fumo dei camini
e la notte al di là del campanile
che attendeva la fune del funambolo.

Partiva il circo la mattina presto
furtivo, con trepestìo di pecorelle,
io poiché, fatti miei, stavo già desto
vedevo svanire il circo e poi le stelle.

THE CIRCUS

A circus is a circus, even a little circus.
My town seemed much more cheerful
of an evening, when, the big top raised,
flags were unfurling in the sky,

when a ding-dong of games and diversions
was making heart and feet go faster
the colors appeared more real
in the new air, it was March, it was evening,

above all the azure, the distant
line of mountains, smoke from chimneys
and night beyond the bell tower
where the tightrope awaited its walker.

The circus would leave in the morning first thing
stealthily, with the footfall of sheep,
me though, my business, I was already up
to watch circus then stars disappearing.

QUESTO È TEMPO DI *HAIKU*

Questo è tempo di *haiku* dice il maestro
tutto il resto *sunt lacrimae rerum*
conta il raggio di luna sul canneto
lasciali perdere, Sacchi e Di Pietro.

THIS IS *HAIKU* TIME ^V

The master says this is *haiku* time
all the rest *sunt lacrimae rerum*
what counts is the moonlight on every reed
Sacchi and Di Pietro you don't need.

RESTA ANCORA QUALCOSA

Resta ancora qualcosa da imparare
dalla pioggia che cade sopra i tetti
dai gatti che la stanno a vedere
in autunno in città:
verticale, come le loro pupille.

SOMETHING REMAINS STILL ✓

Something remains still to learn
from the rain falling over the roofs
from the cats that pause to watch it
in autumn in the city:
vertical, like the pupils of their eyes.

SCALE

Scale
che non portano da nessuna parte
scale
che salgono soltanto per scendere
è difficile orientarsi
nei dintorni del nulla.

STAIRS

Stairs
that don't lead anywhere
stairs
that climb up only to come down
it's difficult to get one's bearings
on nothingness's outskirts.

from *Nella terra di mezzo*

In the Middle Ground (2000)

CAPODANNO A MILANO

Si credeva a Milano che a vedere
per primo un uomo sulla soglia di casa
andando a messa il primo di gennaio
fosse segno di prospero futuro.

Erano figure nere di pastrani
incerte nella nebbia del mattino
sciarpe bianche, cappelli, flosci e duri
rintocchi di bastone, passi lontani.

Or dove siete, uomini augurali?
L'onda lunga del vostro presagio
si frange ancora alla riva degli anni?

Dentro una nebbia tra noi sempre più fitta
mi sembra talvolta intravedere
un volo di profetici mantelli.

NEW YEAR IN MILAN

In Milan they believed that to see
first thing a man at the threshold
going to mass on January first
was the sign of a prosperous future.

They were black figures in greatcoats
indistinct through morning mist
white scarves, hats soft and hard
walking-stick knocks, remote steps.

Where are you now, men of good omen?
the long wave of your augury
breaks still along the years' shore?

In a fog ever thicker between us
from time to time I seem to glimpse
a takeoff of prophetic capes.

ANGELI NERI

C'è un tipo di donna francese
che attira e mette paura
porta un giubbetto di pelle
o farsetti di plastica scura
lavora alle fiere, ai bersagli
vi dà un fucile, mirate, sparate
armigera dunque, o centaura
quando su una moto cavalca
le pareti di un girone di legno
in un turbine di olio bruciato.
L'hanno inventata i giostrai
immagino dica di sì
solo a loro, o ai suoi marsigliesi
io non tento nemmeno
timore? libido? chi sa?
sono cose di anni e anni fa.

BLACK ANGELS

There's a kind of French woman
who attracts and makes you frightened
she wears a little black jacket
or doublets of dark plastic
she works at fairs, on galleries
gives you a rifle, you aim, fire
an armorer then, or centaur
when upon a motorbike she rides
the circular wooden walls
in a whirlwind of burnt petrol.
The roustabouts invented her
I imagine she only says yes
to them, or to her Marseillais
me I don't so much as try
timidity? libido? who knows?
they're things of years and years ago.

GLI INCARICATI

Il mio compagno di Piazza Aquileia
avvocato, con un soprabito grigio
distinto, dal passo affrettato
non ha età, ha una borsa, un cappello
lo rivedo ogni tanto da quando
ho ripreso l'uso del tram
lo vedo di spalle, è di quelli
che vedo sempre di spalle
fa pensare a una vecchia fotografia
di uno che non sai più chi sia.
Quando scende dal 30/29
alto, col suo soprabito a vita
quel mio compagno (cominciava per enne)
mi trasmette l'incarico, so io quale
mentre il tram riprende la corsa
sotto i platani di un altro viale.

THE ENTRUSTED ONES

My companion from Piazza Aquileia
lawyer, with a gray overcoat
distinguished, always in haste
is ageless, has a bag, a hat
I see him now and then since
starting to take the tram again
I see him from behind, he's one
of those I always see from behind
he brings to mind an old photograph
but of who you don't know any more.
When he gets off the 30/29
tall, with his belted overcoat,
that companion of mine (it began with N)
hands me the burden, I know which one
while the tram continues on its way
beneath another avenue of plane trees.

VI ERA QUASI UNA VOCE

Vi era quasi una voce
nel fischio del treno che squarciava
la notte più nera del New Jersey.
Anche oggi questo suono inatteso
così rauco nel cuore della notte
sembra sempre nascondere una voce
pari a un tuono isolato nel pomeriggio
sulle Alpi fiorite di fine estate
a mille altri richiami
a tante risposte senza domanda.

THERE WAS ALMOST A VOICE ✓

There was almost a voice
in the whistle of the train that split
the darker New Jersey night.
Even today this surprising sound
so hoarse within the dead of night
always seems to be hiding a voice
the same as a lone afternoon clap of thunder
on the Alps in flower at summer's end
as a thousand other recalls
as so many replies without question.

IL FORMAGGIO

Sarà bene parlando di un mio modo
di abitare nel mondo del presente
(un sistema spaziale dove scambio
forma e corpo con quanto mi sta attorno
con le cose alle quali vado incontro
per vivere in loro e loro in me)
sarà bene riveli che tal modo
di stare vicino al quotidiano
mi fu chiaro ab initio una mattina
avevo fame era tempo di guerra
da parte a parte guardavo nei buchi
di una fetta sottile di formaggio
così assorto mi sentivo rapito
ed ero un po' di qua un po' di là.

THE CHEESE

It'd be good speaking of my way
to live in the world of the present
(a spatial system where I change
form and body with what's around me
with the things I come across
to live in them and them in me)
it'd be good to reveal such a way
of being near the everyday
became clear to me ab initio one morning
I was hungry it was wartime
from side to side I looked into the holes
of a thin slice of cheese
so distracted I felt myself carried away
and was a bit over here a bit there.

QUANDO CE NE ANDIAMO

Quando ce ne andiamo ti ricordano per un sorriso
per un raro gesto di generosità
per un tic, per la balbuzie, per la loquacità
per la sciarpa bianca o cammello
per la cravatta sbagliata
per l'accento padano
quanto a me ricordatemi come volete
ancor meglio se ne fate a meno, vivete!

WHEN WE GO AWAY

When we go away they recall you for your smile
for a rare generous gesture
for a tic, a stammer, loquacity
for a white or camel scarf
for a misjudged tie
for a Po Valley accent
as for me recall me how you will
better still don't bother, live!

LINEA LOMBARDA

Adoro i pregiudizi, i luoghi comuni
mi piace pensare che in Olanda
ci siano sempre ragazze con gli zoccoli
che a Napoli si suoni il mandolino
che tu mi aspetti un po' in ansia
quando cambio tra Lambrate e Garibaldi.

LOMBARD LINE

Prejudices, commonplaces I adore
I like to think that there are
always girls with clogs in Holland
that they play the mandolin at Naples
that just a bit anxious you await me
when I change between Lambrate and Garibaldi.

IL DOTTOR K RADDOPPIA

Ma lei è mai stato felice nella vita?

come spiegare a questo dottor Kleinkreuz
quel giorno che mettevo in salvo fuori Milano
su un carro a cavalli tra le risaie
i mobili sfollati per la guerra?
il cavallante mi aveva affidato le redini
il carro aveva grandi ruote di camion
avanzava silenzioso come in un altro paese
ero Lucignolo sulle strade del granduca
Iegoruska attraverso la steppa . . .

Proprio come pensavo. Non sa che dire. Sono duecento.

DOCTOR K REDOUBLES

But have you ever been happy in life?

how explain to this Doctor Kleinkreuz
that day I moved outside Milan for safekeeping
on a horse-drawn cart between rice fields
furniture evacuated due to the war?
the driver'd entrusted me with the reins
the wagon had big lorry wheels
it was silently advancing as in another land
I was Lucignolo on the Grand Duke's roads
Iegoruska traversing the steppes . . .

Just as I thought. You've no answer. That's two hundred.

DALLA TERRAZZA

Prima che appaia la luna
sullo schermo del cielo,
navigare sull'internet dei tetti
scoprire alberi e antenne
a Milano, d'agosto.

FROM THE BALCONY ✓

Before the moon appears
on the screen of the sky,
navigate on the internet of roofs
discover trees and aerials
here in Milan, one August.

VI SONO GIORNATE DI VENTO

Vi sono giornate di vento
di fine marzo, di nuvole a strisce:
così allineate sembrano costole
di dinosauri che i cacciatori di fossili
trovano nei sabbioni del Sud Dakota,
ma i miei sauri affondano nell'azzurro
a un nuovo vento, scompaiono un'altra volta.

THERE ARE WINDY DAYS

There are windy days
at March's end, with cloud in stripes:
aligned like so they seem the ribs
of dinosaurs that fossil hunters
find in the sands of South Dakota
but my saurs sink into the blue
with a fresh wind, they disappear once more.

MANI

Mani che ti hanno accarezzato sopra la testa
mani di preti di zie di ortolani
mano del compagno di scuola
che scriveva in inchiostro verde
mani di Berta asciugate dal vento
se appendeva il bucato sopra i fili
larghe mani polacche
che spaccavano legna nell'*Arbeitslager*
mani e dita affusolate
degli amici indiani
mano scarnita
che prendi la penna per firmare
mano che arrivata la sera
accarezzi la gatta più nera.

HANDS

Hands that caressed you on the top of the head
priests' hands aunts' hands fruiterers' hands
hand of the schoolmate
who'd write with green ink
Berta's hands dried in the wind
if she was hanging out washing on lines
broad Polish hands
splitting wood in the *Arbeitslager*
hands and tapering fingers
of our Indian friends
emaciated hand that
takes up the pen to sign
hand that come evening
caresses the much blacker cat.

VORREI PASSARE ALLA STORIA

Vorrei passare alla storia
come un'unità di misura
Watt Volt Faraday
oppure dare il nome a una scala
come Mercalli Fahrenheit Réaumur
la mia sarebbe la scala della noia
al grado uno la pioggia di novembre
al due i locali notturni
al tre, quattro . . . scegliete voi
e così via, fino al nove, me stesso.

I WOULD LIKE TO ENTER HISTORY $\lor$

I would like to enter history
as a unit of measurement
Watt Volt Faraday
or else give the name to a scale
like Mercalli Fahrenheit Réaumur
mine should be the tedium scale
point one November rain
point two the evening haunts
point three, four . . . take your pick
and so on, up to nine, myself.

from *Poesie 1951–2001*

Poems 1951–2001 (2002)

UNA DELLE COSE

Una delle cose che al mattino
mi richiamano al mondo dei tetti
è il riflesso della casa di fronte
nel vetro opaco della mia finestra
aperta da mani femminili
e addossata allo stipite come uno specchio;
facciate s'inseguono a facciate
gialli succedono a gialli
interrotti dal verde di una tenda
dal fianco di un muro in piena luce
come una casa di Delft, ma qui al mattino:
un semplice annuncio del creato
l'azzurro è ora meno disabitato.

ONE OF THE THINGS

One of the things which each morning
recalls me to the world of roofs
is the opposite house reflected
in the opaque glass of my window
opened by womanly hands
and set against the frame like a mirror;
frontage is followed by frontage
yellows succeed upon yellows
interrupted by the green of an awning
from the flank of a wall in full sunlight
like a house in Delft, but here each morning:
a simple announcement of the creation,
the azure is less uninhabited now.

from *L'altra metà*

The Other Half (2004)

E PUR MI GIOVA LA RICORDANZA

a Lucia

Niente è più perso delle figlie
dell'età quando erano bambine
entrò con tutti i suoi capelli biondi
portava un pacco più grande di lei
eppure ricordarsene nel sonno
o al risveglio è una pena gentile
di quelle che fanno provare
qualcosa che ha dell'infinito
e fanno sentire meno amara
la fine, ogni fine a venire.

AND YET THE MEMORY CHEERS ME

to Lucia

Nothing's more lost than your daughters
at the age when they were children
she came in with all her blonde hair
she carried a parcel larger than herself
and yet to recall it in sleep
or at waking is a gentle pain
one of those that makes you feel
something which smacks of the infinite
and they make it taste less bitter,
the end, every end that's on its way.

ALTRA SEDUTA DAL DOTTOR K

Mi capita che annoiandomi a un concerto
distratto dalla gamba lunga e nera
di un pianoforte a coda, di traverso,
mi venga in mente lo stivale da donna
che galleggiava sull'acqua dei Navigli.
«Impossibile» osserva il dottor K
«le donne non portavano stivali
quando lei era ragazzo e c'era ancora
la cerchia scoperta dei Navigli!»
Risponde per me un altro di là del muro:
«Analisi d'accordo, ma l'uno è l'uno!»

OTHER SESSION WITH DOCTOR K

It happens that bored at a concert
distracted by the long black leg
of a grand piano, seen askance,
there comes to mind a woman's boot
afloat on the Navigli's water.
"Impossible" Doctor K observes
"women weren't wearing boots
when you were a lad and the circle
of the Navigli was uncovered still!"
For me another replies beyond the wall:
"Analyses yes, but the one is the one!"

QUARTINE DEL TEMPO LIBERO

Raccolte in alto le redini
guardare le tracce rosso viola
lasciate dagli uccelli di bosco
sulle pietre assolate dei declivi.

Ripiegati i calzoni fino al ginocchio
scoprire conchiglie a bassa marea
fino alla goletta più verde al largo,
nel suo letto di alghe.

Disteso in riva a un torrente
distrarmi al vedere il luccichìo
del contadino che affila la falce
sul ripiano più alto del pendìo.

Appoggiati i gomiti sul davanzale
ascoltare le saracinesche della sera
mentre gli alberi si fanno più scuri
e arrivano i segnali della cena.

Accavallate le gambe stando in poltrona
numerare arabeschi di una stoffa persiana
seduto su una panca tra passeggeri
contare piastrelle della metropolitana.

FREE-TIME QUATRAINS

With reins pulled up
to look at violet-red traces
left by the woodland birds
on sun-baked stones of the slopes.

Trousers rolled to the knees
to find shells at low tide
far as the greener schooner
offshore, on its bed of algae.

Stretched out on a torrent's brink
to be distracted seeing the glitter
of a countryman grinding his scythe
on the hillside's highest terrace.

Elbows resting on the sill
to listen to the shutters at evening
while trees are grown darker
and there come calls to dine.

Legs crossed in the armchair
to count arabesques of Persian cloth
sat on a bench between passengers
to count tiles on the subway line.

HOMO VIATOR

Mi fai andare per labirinti impossibili
tra corridoi di specchi senza uscita
tentare varchi, passaggi invisibili
rimbalzare contro il guard-rail della vita.

Mi sento sabbia e clessidra
pioggia che scende alla finestra
lancetta più lunga sul quadrante
calendario a righe dei miei giorni.

Mi sveglio in stanze bianche dove i mobili
non scricchiolano di notte, alla parete
guardo un quadro di monti senza forma

mi trovo via col pensiero, quasi assente
come il turista che ha sbagliato biglietto
e si rivolge al suo *tour operator*.

HOMO VIATOR

You have me go through impossible mazes
down corridors of mirrors without exit
try openings, invisible passages
bounce off the guardrail of life.

I feel myself sand and clepsydra
rain that descends at the window
longer hand on the clock face
calendar with lines for my days.

I wake up in white rooms where furniture
doesn't creak during the night, on the wall
see a painting of hills with no form

I find myself lost in thought, near absent
like the tourist who's got the ticket wrong
and refers back to his tour operator.

UOMO PENSOSO CON GATTO

a Mairi MacInnes

L'istante del nulla, l'assalto
dell'*es*, dell'*angst, und so weiter*
valgono forse la pena
a patto che passi vicino
con aria di niente il mio gatto
sfiorando la gamba, magari
urtandola con colpi di muso,
poi salti in grembo e allontani
il suolo da sotto le zampe.

PENSIVE MAN WITH CAT

for Mairi MacInnes

The nothing moment, attack
of the *id*, of *angst*, and so forth
they're worth the bother
provided that my cat pass near
with a nonchalant air
brushing my leg, perhaps
bumping it with strokes from his nose,
then leap in my lap and distance
the floor from under his paws.

L'ALTRA METÀ

Non mancano i segnali, anzi in eccesso,
mi sfugge il loro senso, sono troppi?
alla fine mi resta solo un responso:
stai attraversando un incanto a metà.

Basterebbe un piccolo passo, di misura
una luce appena intravista
allora il silenzio sarebbe un altro
sarebbe l'altra metà.

THE OTHER HALF

There's no shortage of signals, an excess even,
their sense escapes me, they're too many?
only one answer is left in the end
you're crossing a half of a spell.

A small step would do, just enough
a light barely glimpsed
the silence would then be an other
would be the other half.

on tradition and discovery

Luciano Erba

— Poetry's adversarial role is best preserved by poets most cautious in the face of innovation.

— The true poet can choose only one tradition to renew.

— In the denial of the past there is always inherent a risk of the commodification, the consumerism of the new.

— The true poet is always an epigone who dwells in language's ancient abode.

— The poet opposes bourgeois society by *conserving* (in symbolic form, by means of myth) anthropological situations on the way to extinction or marginalization. Case by case, he's inclined to adopt a distance not only regarding the media (too easy!) but any other instrument of power, convinced that it is the idiom of the past which will reveal a way towards the idiom of the future.

— Modern society, even if it destroys or secularizes values, can't do anything with the religious, the sense of the sacred: removed from the public sphere, the sacred is reborn in the private, maintaining perennial founding principles in forms that can appear afresh. One could speak at this point of the lay sanctity of the poet.

As appears from these six preliminary reflections (but one could add others, of course), I have always felt the need to keep a distance from such poetic "novelties" as I came into conflict with in the course of my by now long career. Born in 1922, growing up during two decades under the sign of the fascist regime's triumphalist rhetoric, I soon began to feel unease with the "system" and as soon as possible, in the situation of uncertainty occurring after the September 1943 Armistice, I went the mountain way, as they used to say then, so as to choose freedom in a neutral neighbor state. On my return, after the victory of the Allies and the consequent liberation of northern Italy, in the spring of 1945 I found a cultural climate not that different from the one I'd left behind, under the sign of a new rhetoric, ideological conformism, the most advanced "transformism." Those involved with literature were expected to "reflect" the changed times of the country, as did the political parties, the free exchange of ideas, the means of communication (one didn't speak of the *media* as yet). But 1945 was not a literary date, even if there were attempts to make it pass for one. It's for reasons entirely exterior or instrumental that one tends to reveal a concomitance between the great historical events and the modest, gradual "turns" of literature. At the most, one could instead say, in this case, that our political and military events during the years 1940–45, events which ended as we know, determined the disappearance, or almost, of our fragile national values, favoring the emergence of many regional and municipal distinctivenesses that the culture of those twenty years had thought to throw into the attic.

As we know, the real poetry of that time defended itself against the rhetoric of the regime by concealing itself in the current of what could appear pure literature but which also, such was hermeticism, kept in step with the most advanced experiences of European writing. To the many establishment versifiers was left the task of "singing" works and deeds fed to the masses by state propaganda: Roman marshes, colonial campaigns, and other applauded themes destined to disappear from the scene at the fall of the regime. Hermeticism, as was right, survived and remained for years the poetic model to which the true poets of the succeeding generations made reference, while there remained not a trace of the entirely fanciful attempts to "sing" (yet again!) the new historical times in a realistic register or, as they preferred to say, "neorealist," chasing after poetic material in its most overexposed and theatrical aspect (social ruptures, popular struggles . . .). The true return to the real was in the attempts of the young post-hermetic poets, who, without renouncing the revelatory power of the word, rediscovered the absolute in the most discreet and above all concrete signals of being, and its vibrations.

The so-called neo-avant-garde (the '60s) did not want, though, to recognize themselves in this post-hermeticism of an often Montalean stamp;

with their clamorous and well-programmed linguistic transgressions, they didn't find it difficult to gain the favor of a little limelight. As with all the functionaries of "isms," the neo-avant-garde would no less quickly exit from the scene; but they at least, and for this we must thank them, did end up completely obscuring the neorealism or superficial realism—which we've already mentioned—of other new "singers" and versifiers inclined to think that to be a poet it's enough to take on the civil or social burden simply expressed via the call to causes or the defense of values which are in themselves extraneous, even if the noblest, to the more authentic logics of poetry, to its DNA.

After this alternation of successive appearances and dissolutions we attend today to the silence of group poetics, while what seems to be preferred is an undifferentiated immersion in the quotidian and the private. We are living through a season of interchangeability; we have a free fluctuation of money and small change—perhaps awaiting a single currency, if it ever comes. Will it be better? Won't this mean the return of an nth specific poetics, with the inevitable requirement to outlaw what is considered non-specific, not poetry, worse, to speak again of project making?

While awaiting the improbable advent of a poetic Euro, I'll transcribe from my workshop ledger some points connected with this subject:

— Simplicity: it's the most difficult path. Defending yourself against an artful simplicity, quite ridiculous, against writing as a voluntary gesture of simplification that intends to cast light *sic et simpliciter* on spaces that in their nature cannot stand the light. To reach authentic simplicity one moves through the forest of cultural stimuli, reactivating the sense of words, not caring if one ends up by being different from what readers would expect one to be. As Pasternak wrote: "being connected to all that exists / frequenting the future in everyday life / one cannot but in the end incur as in a heresy, / an unbelievable simplicity" ["Things of great worth shall come to pass . . ." (1931)].

— Drift. Eternal point of departure from a place arrived at, from a positional payoff. The subject that abandons itself to the current, to wandering, to elsewhere, is chosen by the route, doesn't choose it, just as a dreamer is chosen by the dreams that he produces in the night, as the sailor in a tempest no longer controls the sails and the helm, but is chosen by the currents and the waters. Very often, if not always, rather than situating himself, the poet is situated, quickly altering the new situation, his own journey, his own figure of the traveler.

— Importance of *objects*. Whether you're dealing with enlarged details, or with Gulliverized scales, even if we'd better not speak of gracious miniatures. I recover in this way the vision of adolescence, at least so I believe. It is in the comparison with the little, in the discovery of what had always escaped the attention, that I encounter the most diverse and unexpected surprises of being. Attention is always altered, conditioned by intentionality; by nature it misses the mysterious. I prefer the deserts of inattention, the haystack, not the needle.

— Objective correlative. T. S. Eliot, of course. Objects are expressive of what the "I" cannot say or does not know how to say about itself; they reroute, they "dribble" the grammatical "I." An invariability is established, then, between a thing and its contrary, an equivalence between choice and renunciation of choice, between word and silence, between a form and a content which exchange roles. Poetry can in this way be reversed like a glove: it's unidimensional. The sign refers back to itself, like Alice's playing cards or the canvases of Warhol: behind them there is nothing, but precisely because I don't want to say anything, I say something.

— The any-old cosmic. In the appearances of the everyday there are things that stick out. I grasp them whatever they are: eternal dimensions, forms at their highest level of abstraction, simply geometrical-like lines, half-lines, diagonals, curves, triangles, squares, circles, or their shadows on the ground, or their imprints in the sky. For a moment, it seems then that a system of closure is unblocked, a way is opened . . . Are they railway tracks or two lines at equal distance the one from the other? Is it a house on the corner of two streets or a triangular prism? A group of housing blocks or rather squares, or trapezoids? What to say of the outlines of the room, of the corners dissolving to become more essential before sleep takes possession of our senses?

— Again on the theme of any indefinite space. Border country, for example, countries of contradictions, undecided regions, uncertain places, non-places: without name, without flag they go by unnoticed. They are the last *terrae incognitae* which remain to be explored: roads with no prestige, sleeping cities, districts neither working-class nor residential, aggregations of whatever cells, where there live the silent majority of people and blades of grass, stones, and clouds. In this impersonal universe, persons and things until now familiar and interchangeable all of a sudden become bearers of the new. I discover them as if for the first time; I experience a true sensation of existence. The whole being receives a start, "their" being, my being, the city.

— The same is true of time. There are moments that are any moment, just as there are objects that are any object. There is the same amount of truth and mystery in moments before an event as in the event itself; in the second in which a leaf is disturbed by the wind, or in which you hear the cry of a passing bird, as in the instant immediately after the bridge mined by partisans will explode; in the moment you throw the dice, or in that of the cannon fire, even if you are aiming from the *Aurora* at the Winter or the Middle Season Palace. In contrast to the *suspense* preceding the decisive moment, this one fades before fractions of time that, since they don't belong to history, allow you to glimpse the possibility of another dimension.

— Poet and *orator* are the same thing. Poetry is a gift born from the grace of inspiration, a seed which nevertheless will have to develop, to grow roots, blossom with help from the same *vis*, only apparently less involuntary and adventurous than was the image's lightning or a chance series of words: it will be a *poetic reworking* in that kind of Intensive Care for initial inspiration which is the entirely secret worktable where the author adds and subtracts, intervenes and changes, puts in a rhyme and starts a new line, cuts what's out of tune, reveals and conceals, clarifies the doubts and doubts the certainties, modulates opacities and transparencies, etc. etc., the art, in a word, or *tékhne* as the Greeks used to say.

— If it's true that the text which we consider definitive represents nothing but the interruption of the creative process, an organism whose growth stops, we have to resign ourselves to the law that the text will always be *in progress* and our *ne varietur* is a convenient monumentalization, recalling the paradox that what is not said always has a stronger presence than what is.

— Rhyme, meter. For the above reasons, a sought-for rhyme is differently, but not less, poetic than a spontaneous "given" rhyme. We can even say that the unconscious, whether private or collective, and never entirely repressed, the intended in that case, the progressive deepening or lightening of the theme, the renouncing and the enriching of the dictated, come into play as creative and selective elements passing through the enchanted mesh of rhyme, assonance, of the traditional metrical structures. It's above all the project, when present, that cannot escape the games of chance. A certain rhyme, which for apparently futile reasons, for example literary cunning, has to replace the one which "grace" had suggested earlier, in the end reveals itself as absolutely decisive, as the only one which is able to change entirely for the better (but does it really change it?) the meaning of the whole poem. Curiously the newcomer, although born in the workshop rather than on the field, is welcomed by the text as like a prodigal son who has been found once more.

notes

ANOTHER CITY

"cervi volanti": the translation offered with the advice of the poet is "kites" — meaning not the large bird of prey, but the object for flying in the park.

THE GALLANT GENT

Rosalba Carriera: a miniaturist and official portrait painter (Venice 1675–1757).

IN THE PARK AT VERSAILLES

"sub tegmine fagi": "under the shadow of the beech tree," from Virgil, *Eclogue* 1, line 1.
"opus Lenotri": André Le Nôtre (1613–1700), the French architect who designed the park at Versailles.

FEELING OF TIME

"Sentimento del tempo" is also the title, alluded to ironically by Erba, of Giuseppe Ungaretti's 1933 collection of poems.
"R. G.": Renato Ghiotto, a Veronese writer.
"Mahori": the word for a musical style of southeast Asia adopted to evoke the South Seas, and drawing upon an uncertain memory of a song heard on the radio in the dormitory of a work camp during World War II. The rain also recalls the same period from the author's life.

A HEALTH RESORT

a "Ph. J." : Philippe Jaccottet (1925–), the French poet.

THE BEAUTIFUL COUNTRY

In the Italian poem, "Honeste" is spelled with an "H" to suggest the old-fashioned manners of the great uncles.

WITH DOCTOR K

"Mariahilfe": actually, Mariahilfer, indicating the Vienna West railway station.

"ce blanc si tendre de plâtre / sous un ciel de vent d'ouest / sali par les cheminées d'hiver": "this so tender plaster white / under a sky of west wind / dirtied by the chimneys of winter."

"ce blanc des cuisses des filles / quand elles quittent leurs bas noirs dans un meublé": "this white of girls' thighs / when they leave their black stockings in a hotel room."

"Adler": Alfred Adler (1870–1937), with Freud and Jung a founding father of psychoanalysis.

UNDECIDED

"Undecided": the name of a swing number from the 1930s.

A FIRST-DEGREE EQUATION

"Biffi Scala": a fashionable café in Milan.

LAND AND SEA

"Madame Lenormant": an invented name meant to evoke Le Havre and Normandy.

Giordano Bruno (1548–1600) was an epistemological philosopher and propagandist for the Copernican version of the universe, burned alive in Rome as a heretic.

"nominatim": "namely."

De la Causa Principio e Uno (1584) is a proto-pantheistic dialogue in which the world's various appearances are defined as aspects of a single, immobile, and eternal being.

BOOK OF HOURS

The poet is Henri Michaux in his book *Ecuador* (1929). Erba's translation of his "La Cordillera de los Andes" was collected in *Dei cristalli naturali e altri versi tradotti 1950–1990* (1991).

"quincunxes": trees planted in a five-spot pattern as on dice.

"lilliputian railways": small-gauge railroads offer a glimpse of Machu Picchu, also hinted at in the "sugarloaf peaks" of the following line.

CAIN AND THE THORNS

"Cain and the Thorns": that's to say, the moon; cf. Dante, *Inferno* XX, 126, and *Paradiso* II, 51.

DIGNUS EST INTRARE

"Dignus est intrare": "He deserves to enter," a solecism spoken by the chorus in act 3, the burlesque of a doctor's degree ceremony, in Molière's *Le Malade imaginaire*.

HIPPOGRAMS & METAHIPPOGRAMS OF THE PAINTER GIOVANOLA

The works of Gianluigi Giovanola (1924–) include pairs of variously imagined horse-shapes that are the inspiration for this poem.
"Ryukyu": an archipelago including Okinawa to the south of Japan where they practice a particular type of free wrestling, more violent than judo.

IN THE IVORY TOWER

"in aeternum": "in the ever after."
"bersaglieri": "sharp-shooters"—specifically, Italian soldiers whose march is a run and who wear distinctive black-feathered caps.
"lamed zayin aleph": letters from the Hebrew alphabet suggested by the hair falling across D's forehead.

VANITAS VARIETATUM

"Vanitas Varietatum": "Vanity of Varieties," a play on the biblical "Vanitas vanitatum" (Vanity of vanities).
"the bersaglieri / once more enter Trieste": the poet explains that he was thinking of the agitated movements of characters in old silent movies.

FAR BEYOND THE FROZEN SEAS

The Italian title is line 8 of verse 18 in canto 4 of Ariosto's *Orlando Furioso*.

THE INATTENTIVE

Monte Cavallo: according to the poet, an imaginary place whose name is meant to give the idea of a horse's back.

INCOMPATIBILITY

"Oldani": a common Milanese name suggesting solid ordinary people.

"ninettes": prostitutes, referring to Carlo Porta's poem "La Ninetta del verzee." The "verzee" was the vegetable market in Milan.

SUPER FLUMINA

"Super flumina": "On the rivers," the beginning of Psalm 136 (137 in some Bibles) on the Babylonian exile.

"Triangulations": explained by the author as indirect shots in billiards and thus, by analogy, ways of proceeding by indirection in politics and other walks of life.

"Ixion": a mythical king said to have engendered centaurs by lying with a cloud that Zeus had made to appear like Hera; as a punishment, he was bound to a wheel by Zeus and whirls forever in Hades.

"counter-Danaides": the Danaides are girls doomed forever to fill urns with water that disappears; these "counter-Danaides" are condemned to bail out interminably.

Adda: a large river in Lombardy.

The "ignorance" called a "lesser evil" is the "docta ignorantia" of Socrates: that I know I know nothing.

AEROSTATICS

"*à double face*": it can also be worn with the lining outside.

MY FORTIES

The English title is given in this form to indicate the poet's forties, not the 1940s.

"hills of the Gods": clearly, in this context, the protruberances on the palm of the hand (c.f. above, the "Life Line"), called in palmistry the Mount of Jove, the Mount of Saturn, etc.

BETWEEN SPACE AND TIME

"Per kelle fini": "within those borders," words which appear in the so-called *Carta Capuana*, the first known record of the Italian language (A.D. 960). "*Per*" can have, here, the sense of an expletive. There is, officially anyway, no K in the Italian alphabet.

"*maybe-costing-great-pain*": the author notes that in the dear old days of rote learning one would keep in mind the sequence of Alpine mountain chains (Maritime, Cozie, Graie, Pennine . . .) with the Italian equivalents of these words, which have been rendered with the same initial letters as a gesture of fidelity.

RELOCATION

"the pettineuses the buffé the contrabuffé": French names for pieces of furniture used by the Lombard cabinet makers from the Brianza area near Milan.

BARCELONA BALTIMORE . . .

The "album raffaello" is an especially good brand of drawing paper.

WHY NOT ME

"Tanaro": a river in the Piedmont.

FESTIVAL OF NATIONS

"the latin sister": France.
Colorno and Rubiera are in Emilia; the setting is from Stendhal's *The Charterhouse of Parma.*

NEW METHODS OF DOCTOR K

"Volta Park": a fairground in Milan.

MAILAND

"Mailand": Milan in German.
The "fabbrica italiana di ghiaccio artificiale" is "enough / to make us laugh" because its acronym "figa" spells the Milanese dialect word for the female genital.
"*krapfen* and *kipfeln*": Italian loan-words from German, both characteristically beginning with K, which might be rendered as "doughnuts and pastries."

IDÉE FIXE

"*antiquam exquirite matrem*": "search for the old mother"; Virgil, *Aeneid* III, 96.

SEVEN AND A HALF

"Sette e mezzo" is the name of a card game in which seven and a half points is the winning score. The poem combines various different "seven and a halfs" (age, time of day, months of the year) to instance a child's magical understanding of the world.

ISTRIA

"Albona": Italian name for a town now in Slovenia.

SUITE AMERICANA

"the diagonal": Broadway.

"N. B.": the city of New Brunswick, New Jersey.

QUARTIERE SOLARI

"*Umanitaria*": council housing built in derelict areas of Milan.

I LIVE THIRTY METERS FROM THE GROUND

"Torriani," "Erba": leading old Milanese families. The poet shares only his surname with the latter.

"Baron Münchhausen": the eponymous personage in R. E. Raspe's tales of 1785 is a teller of fantastic stories, including one in which he travels through the sky on a cannonball.

IF IT WEREN'T

"que le blanc ne se casse": that the white wine, or champagne, doesn't stay too long in the cold, running the risk that it alter or freeze.

IF THIS IS ALL . . .

"the new clerks' treason": alluding to Julian Benda's *La Trahison des clercs* (1928).

A VISIT TO CALEPPIO

Caleppio is in flat rice-growing country on the edge of Milan.

"London Calling": the phrase made famous by the opening words of the BBC radio broadcast to enemy or occupied territories during World War II—"This is London calling."

"There are more things in heaven and earth, Horatio, / Than are dreamt of in your philosophy": *Hamlet,* act I, scene 5, ll. 166–67.

LA VIDA ES . . .

See "La caduta" by Giuseppe Parini. *La Vida Es . . .* is from Calderón de la Barca's *La vida es sueño* ("Life is a dream").

MOTUS IN FINE VELOCIOR

"Motus in fine velocior": motion accelerates towards an end.
"Inter": Internazionale Football Club Milano.

ANY OLD COSMOS

"*Trabant*": a cheap, mass-produced car built in Warsaw Pact countries during the Cold War.

GENIUS LOCI

Dino Campana (1885–1932), author of the *Canti orfici*, was born at Marradi in Tuscany.

ONLY SIGNS?

INRI: Iesus Nazarenus Rex Iudaeorum, the initials that Pontius Pilate had nailed to the cross.
SPQR: Senatus Populusque Romani, the legislative body of ancient Rome.
Of the poem's last line, the author notes: "I'm referring to '. . . the Word within / The world and for the world,' in T. S. Eliot's *Ash-Wednesday*, V; in March 1939 at Corpus Christi College, Cambridge, the poet gave the three lectures on *The Idea of a Christian Society*."

DASEIN

"*Dasein*": a term meaning approximately "being here," found in the writings of philosophers such as Hegel and Heidegger.

RAILWAY SUITE

"1942" was written in that year and appeared in the *Meridiano di Roma* on 8 November 1942 in a section that published the work of young poets. The other two poems are from the 1980s. "1943" refers to the Republic of Salò (1943–45), a fascist puppet state in northern Italy with Mussolini as its head. The poet escaped to Switzerland to avoid conscription into its armed forces.
"the turn-box nun": Erba's Italian is derived from the French *soeur tourière*, a nun from a not-closed order entrusted with the conducting of relations between a closed convent and the outside world.

CHASING VITTORIO S ON THE ZENNA ROAD

"Vittorio S": Vittorio Sereni (1913–83). The allusion is to his poem "Strada di Zenna" ("Zenna Road") from *Frontiera* (1941).

THE CIRCUS

This poem is a free compression of a poem by Andrea Zanzotto, "Dolcezza. Carezza. Piccoli schiaffi in quiete," from *Il Galateo in bosco* (1978).

THIS IS *HAIKU* TIME

"Sacchi and Di Pietro": Arigo Sacchi was a coach of the Italian soccer team and Antonio Di Pietro a judge in the political corruption trials of the early 1990s. They are, though, as the poem suggests, the sorts of names created by one time and forgotten by a subsequent one.

THE CHEESE

"ab initio": from the start.

LOMBARD LINE

The "Linea lombarda" is a name given by Luciano Anceschi to a group of poets from Milan and its surroundings such as Sereni and Erba.
"Lambrate and Garibaldi": train stations in Milan.

DOCTOR K REDOUBLES

"Lucignolo": the bad boy who invites Pinocchio to "The Land of Toys."
"Iegoruska": the protagonist of Chekhov's story *The Steppes*.

AND YET THE MEMORY CHEERS ME

The Italian title is from lines 10–11 of Leopardi's "Alla luna."

HOMO VIATOR

"*Homo viator*": traveling man.

LUCIANO ERBA was born in Milan in 1922. He studied French, graduating from the Catholic University of Milan in 1947. His research has been in the literary history of the early seventeenth century, in nineteenth-century symbolism, and twentieth-century literature. Erba first taught in schools and then at various universities including Bari, Bologna, Udine, Verona, and the Catholic University of Milan. Though he has lived most of his life in the city of his birth, there have been extended periods spent abroad: in Switzerland during the latter part of World War II, where he was interned, from 1947 to 1950 in Paris, where he taught Italian, and from 1963 to 1966 in the United States, where he was first a visiting, then associate professor of comparative literature.

Erba made his literary debut with *Linea K* (1951). His numerous subsequent collections include *Il male minore* (1960), *Il prato più verde* (1977), *Il nastro di Moebius* (1980), *L'ippopotamo* (1989), *L'ipotesi circense* (1995), and *Nella terra di mezzo* (2000)—all collected in *Poesie 1951–2001* (2002). He is known too for his translations of Blaise Cendrars, Pierre Reverdy, Henri Michaux, Francis Ponge, Thom Gunn, and other French and English poets. Erba has published a collection of stories, *Françoise* (1982), and, with Piero Chiara, edited an anthology of new postwar Italian poets, *Quarta generazione* (1954). He has been awarded many of Italy's most prestigious literary prizes, including the Viareggio (1980), the Bagutta (1988), the Librex-Guggenheim "Eugenio Montale" (1989), the Italian Pen Club (1995), and the Pasolini in 2005.

PETER ROBINSON was born in Salford, Lancashire (UK) in 1953. He grew up in Liverpool and holds degrees from the universities of York and Cambridge. During the 1970s and 1980s he taught for various universities and other institutions in Britain, and was involved in organizing a number of Cambridge International Poetry Festivals. Since 1989, he has been a professor of English Literature in Japan, at present in Kyoto, where he lives with his Italian wife and their two daughters.

He is internationally known for his poetry (Cheltenham Prize, 1988), his translations (Poetry Book Society recommendation, 2002), and his literary criticism. Among his many publications are *Selected Poems* (2003), *Twentieth Century Poetry: Selves and Situations* (2005), and *Talk about Poetry: Conversations on the Art* (2006). The University of Chicago Press has recently published *Selected Poetry and Prose of Vittorio Sereni*, edited and translated by Peter Robinson and Marcus Perryman. A book of critical studies, *The Salt Companion to Peter Robinson*, edited by Adam Piette and Katy Price, appeared in October 2006.

THE LOCKERT LIBRARY OF POETRY IN TRANSLATION

George Seferis: Collected Poems (1924–1955), translated, edited, and introduced by
Edmund Keeley and Philip Sherrard

Collected Poems of Lucio Piccolo, translated and edited by Brian Swann and
Ruth Feldman

C. P. Cavafy: Selected Poems, translated by Edmund Keeley and Philip Sherrard and
edited by George Savidis

Benny Andersen: Selected Poems, translated by Alexander Taylor

Selected Poetry of Andrea Zanzotto, edited and translated by Ruth Feldman
and Brian Swann

Poems of René Char, translated and annotated by Mary Ann Caws and
Jonathan Griffin

Selected Poems of Tudor Arghezi, translated by Michael Impey
and Brian Swann

"The Survivor" and Other Poems, by Tadeusz Rózewicz, translated and introduced by
Magnus J. Krynski and Robert A. Maguire

"Harsh World" and Other Poems, by Angel González, translated by Donald D. Walsh

Ritsos in Parentheses, translated and introduced by Edmund Keeley

Salamander: Selected Poems of Robert Marteau, translated by Anne Winters

Angelos Sikelianos: Selected Poems, translated and introduced by Edmund Keeley
and Philip Sherrard

Dante's "Rime," translated by Patrick S. Diehl

Selected Later Poems of Marie Luise Kaschnitz, translated by Lisel Mueller

Osip Mandelstam's "Stone," translated and introduced by Robert Tracy

The Dawn Is Always New: Selected Poetry of Rocco Scotellaro, translated by
Ruth Feldman and Brian Swann

Sounds, Feelings, Thoughts: Seventy Poems by Wisława Szymborska, translated
and introduced by Magnus J. Krynski and Robert A. Maguire

The Man I Pretend To Be: "The Colloquies" and Selected Poems of Guido Gozzano,
translated and edited by Michael Palma, with an introductory essay
by Eugenio Montale

D'Après Tout: Poems by Jean Follain, translated by Heather McHugh

Songs of Something Else: Selected Poems of Gunnar Ekelöf, translated by
Leonard Nathan and James Larson

The Little Treasury of One Hundred People, One Poem Each, compiled by
Fujiwara No Sadaie and translated by Tom Galt

The Ellipse: Selected Poems of Leonardo Sinisgalli, translated by W. S. Di Piero

The Difficult Days, by Robert Sosa, translated by Jim Lindsey

Hymns and Fragments, by Friedrich Hölderlin, translated and introduced by
Richard Sieburth